ISBN 978-1-331-24748-7
PIBN 10163976

1 MONTH OF
FREE
READING

at

www.ForgottenBooks.com

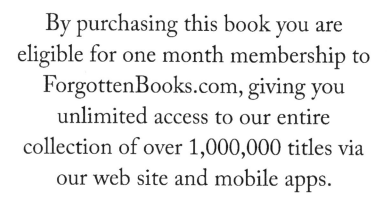

By purchasing this book you are eligible for one month membership to ForgottenBooks.com, giving you unlimited access to our entire collection of over 1,000,000 titles via our web site and mobile apps.

To claim your free month visit:

www.forgottenbooks.com/free163976

English
Français
Deutsche
Italiano
Español
Português

www.forgottenbooks.com

Mythology Photography **Fiction**
Fishing Christianity **Art** Cooking
Essays Buddhism Freemasonry
Medicine **Biology** Music **Ancient**
Egypt Evolution Carpentry Physics
Dance Geology **Mathematics** Fitness
Shakespeare **Folklore** Yoga Marketing
Confidence Immortality Biographies
Poetry **Psychology** Witchcraft
Electronics Chemistry History **Law**
Accounting **Philosophy** Anthropology
Alchemy Drama Quantum Mechanics
Atheism Sexual Health **Ancient History**
Entrepreneurship Languages Sport
Paleontology Needlework Islam
Metaphysics Investment Archaeology
Parenting Statistics Criminology
Motivational

SOCIOLOGY FOR THE SOUTH,

OR THE

FAILURE OF FREE SOCIETY.

BY GEORGE FITZHUGH.

THE THING THAT HAS BEEN, IT IS THAT WHICH SHALL BE; AND THAT WHICH IS DONE IS THAT WHICH SHALL BE DONE; AND THERE IS NO NEW THING UNDER THE SUN.—Ecc. 1: 9.

Naturam expelles furca, tamen usque recurret.---Horace.

RICHMOND, VA.
A. MORRIS, PUBLISHER.
1854.

C. H. WYNNE, PRINTER, RICHMOND.

TO THE PEOPLE OF THE SOUTH.

We dedicate this little work to you, because it is a zealous and honest effort to promote your peculiar interests. Society has been so quiet and contented in the South—it has suffered so little from crime or extreme poverty, that its attention has not been awakened to the revolutionary tumults, uproar, mendicity and crime of free society. Few are aware of the blessings they enjoy, or of the evils from which they are exempt.

From some peculiarity of taste, we have for many years been watching closely the perturbed workings of free society. Its crimes, its revolutions, its sufferings and its beggary, have led us to investigate its past history, as well as to speculate on its future destiny. This pamphlet has been hastily written, but is the result of long observation, some research and much reflection. Should it contain suggestions that will enlist abler pens to show that free society is a failure and its philosophy false, our highest ambition will be gratified. Believing our positions on these subjects to be true, we feel sanguine they are destined to final vindication and triumph. We should have written a larger work, had not our inexperience in authorship warned

us that we had better await the reception of this. We
may again appear in the character of writer before the
public; but we shall not intrude, and would prefer that
others should finish the work which we have begun.
Treating subjects novel and difficult of comprehension,
we have designedly indulged in iteration; for we pre-
ferred offending the ear and the taste of the reader,
to confounding or confusing him by insufficient elaboration.   In truth, fine finish and rotundity are not
easily attained in what is merely argumentative and
controversial.

On all subjects of social science, Southern men, from
their position, possess peculiar advantages when they
undertake discussion.   History, past and cotemporaneous, informs them of all the phenomena of other
forms of society, and they see every day around them
the peculiarities and characteristics of slave society, of
which little is to be learned from books. The ancients
took it for granted that slavery was right, and never
attempted to justify it.   The moderns assume that it
is wrong, and forthwith proceed to denounce it.   The
South can lose nothing, and may gain, by the discussion.
She has, up to this time, been condemned without a
hearing.

With respect, your fellow-citizen,

GEO. FITZHUGH.

PREFACE.

We hesitated some time in selecting the title of our work. We did not like to employ the newly-coined word Sociology. We could, however, find none other in the whole range of the English language, that would even faintly convey the idea which we wished to express. We looked to the history of the term. We found that within the last half century, disease, long lurking in the system of free society, had broken out into a hundred open manifestations. Thousands of authors and schemers, such as Owen, Louis Blanc and Fourier, had arisen, proposing each a different mode of treatment for the disease which all confessed to exist. Society had never been in such a state before. New exigencies in its situation had given rise to new ideas, and to a new philosophy. This new philosophy must have a name, and as none could be found ready-made to suit the occasion, the term Sociology was compounded, of hybrid birth, half Greek and half Latin, as the technical appellative of the new-born science. In Europe, the term is familiar as "household words." It grates harshly, as yet, on Southern ears, because to us it is new and superfluous—the disease of which it treats being unknown amongst us. But as our book is intended to prove that we are indebted to domestic slavery for our happy exemption from the social afflictions that have originated this philosophy, it became necessary and appropriate that we should employ this new word in our title. The fact that, before the institution of Free Society, there was no such term, and that it is not in use in slave countries, now, shows pretty clearly that Slave Society, ancient and modern, has ever been in so happy a condition, so exempt from ailments, that no doctors have arisen to treat it of its complaints, or to propose remedies for their cure. The term, therefore, is not only appropriate to the subject and the occasion, but pregnantly suggestive of facts and arguments that sustain our theory.

CHAPTER I.

Political economy is the science of free society. Its theory and its history alike establish this position. Its fundamental maxims, *Laissez-faire* and "*Pas trop gouverner*," are at war with all kinds of slavery, for they in fact assert that individuals and peoples prosper most when governed least. It is not, therefore, wonderful that such a science should not have been believed or inculcated whilst slavery was universal. Roman and Greek masters, feudal lords and Catholic priests, if conscientious, must have deemed such maxims false and heritical, or if unconscientious, would find in their self-interest sufficient reasons to prevent their propagation. Accordingly we find no such maxims current, no such science existing, until slavery and serfdom were extinct and Catholicism maimed and crippled, in the countries that gave them birth. Men belonging to the higher classes of society, and who neither feel nor apprehend the ills of penury or privation, are very apt to think little of those ills, and less of the class who suffer them. Especially is this the case with unobservant, abstract thinkers and closet scholars, who deal with little of the world and see less of it. Such men judge of mankind, their progress and their happiness, by the few specimens subjected to the narrow range of their experience and observation. After the abolition of feudalism and Catholicism, an immense amount of unfettered talent, genius, industry and capital, was brought into the field of free competition. The immediate result was, that all those who possessed either of those advantages prospered as they had never prospered before, and rose in social position and intelligence. At the same time, and from the same causes, the aggregate wealth of society, and probably its aggregate intelligence, were rapidly increased. Such was no doubt part of the effects of unfettering the limbs, the minds and consciences of men. It was the only part of those effects that scholars and philosophers saw or heeded. Here was something new under the sun, which refuted and rebuked the wisdom of Solomon. Up to this time, one-half of mankind had been little better than chattels belonging to the other half. A central power, with branches radiating throughout the civilized world, had trammeled men's consciences, dictated their religious faith, and prescribed the forms and modes of worship. All this was done away with, and the new world just started into existence was certainly making rapid progress, and seemed to the ordinary observer to be very happy. About such a world, nothing was to be found in books. Its social, its industrial and its moral phenomena, seemed to be as beautiful as they were novel. They needed, however, description, classification and arrangement. Men's social relations and moral duties were quite different under a system of universal liberty and equality of rights, from what they had been in a state of subordination and dependence on the one side, and of power, authority and protection on the other. The reciprocal duties and obligations of master and slave, of lord and vassal, of priest and layman, to each other, were altogether unlike those that should be practiced between the free and equal citizens of regenerated society. Men needed a moral guide, a new philosophy of ethics; for neither the sages of the Gentiles, nor the Apostles of Christianity, had foreseen or provided for the great light which was now to burst upon the world. Moses, and Solomon, and Paul, were silent as Socrates, Plato and Aristotle, as to this social Millenium, and the moral duties and obligations it would bring in its train.

Until now, industry had been controlled and directed by a few minds. Monopoly in its every form had been rife. Men were suddenly called on to walk alone, to act and work for themselves without guide, advice or control from superior

authority. In the past, nothing like it had occurred; hence no assistance could be derived from
books. The prophets themselves had overlooked
or omitted to tell of the advent of this golden
era, and were no better guides than the historians
and philosophers. A philosophy that should guide
and direct industry was equally needed with a
philosophy of morals. The occasion found and
made the man. For writing a one-sided philosophy, no man was better fitted than Adam Smith.
He possessed extraordinary powers of abstraction,
analysis and generalization. He was absent, secluded and unobservant. He saw only that pros-
perons and progressive portion of society whom
liberty or free competition benefitted, and mistook
its effects on them for its effects on the world.
He had probably never heard the old English
adage, "Every man for himself, and Devil take
the hindmost." This saying comprehends the
whole philoscphy, moral and economical, of the
"Wealth of Nations." But he and the political
economists who have succeeded him, seem never
to have dreamed that there would have been any
"hindmost." There can never be a wise moral
philosopher, or a sound philosophy, till some one
arises who sees and comprehends all the "things
in heaven and earth." Philosophers are the most
abstracted, secluded, and least observant of men.
Their premises are always false, because they see

but few facts; and hence their conclusions must
also be false. Plato and Aristotle have to-day
as many believers as Smith, Paley or Locke, and
between their times a hundred systems have arisen,
flourished for a time, and been rejected. There
is not a true moral philosophy, and from the nature of things there never can be. Such a philosophy has to discover first causes and ultimate
effects, to grasp infinitude, to deal with eternity
at both ends. Human presumption will often attempt this, but human intellect can never achieve
it. *We* shall build up no system, attempt to
account for nothing, but simply point out what
is natural and universal, and humbly try to justify the ways of God to man.

Adam Smith's philosophy is simple and comprehensive, (*teres et rotundus.*) Its leading and
almost its only doctrine is, that individual well-
being and social and national wealth and prosperity will be best promoted by each man's eagerly
pursuing his own selfish welfare unfettered and
unrestricted by legal regulations, or governmental
prohibitions, farther than such regulations may be
necessary to prevent positive crime. That some
qualifications of this doctrine will not be found
in his book, we shall not deny; but this is his
system. It is obvious enough that such a governmental policy as this doctrine would result in,
would stimulate energy, excite invention and in-

dustry, and bring into livelier action, genius, skill
and talent. It had done so before Smith wrote,
and it was no doubt the observation of those
effects that suggested the theory. His friends
and acquaintances were of that class, who, in the
war of the wits to which free competition invited,
were sure to come off victors. His country, too,
England and Scotland, in the arts of trade and
in manufacturing skill, was an over-match for
the rest of the world. International free trade
would benefit his country as much as social free
trade would benefit his friends. This was his
world, and had it been the only world his philosophy would have been true. But there was
another and much larger world, whose misfortunes, under his system, were to make the fortunes of his friends and his country. A part of
that world, far more numerous than his friends
and acquaintance was at his door, they were the
unemployed poor, the weak in mind or body,
the simple and unsuspicious, the prodigal, the dis-
sipated, the improvident and the vicious. *Laissez-faire* and *pas trop gouverner* suited not them;
one portion of them needed support and protection; the other, much and rigorous government.
Still they were fine subjects out of which the
astute and designing, the provident and avari-
cions, the cunning, the prudent and the industrious might make fortunes in the field of free

competition. Another portion of the world which Smith overlooked, were the countries with which England traded, covering a space many hundred times larger than England herself. She was daily growing richer, more powerful and intellectual, by her trade, and the countries with which she traded poorer, weaker, and more ignorant. Since the vast extension of trade, consequent on the discoveries of Columbus and Vasco de Gama, the civilized countries of Europe which carried on this trade had greatly prospered, but the savages and barbarians with whom they traded had become more savage and barbarous or been exterminated. Trade is a war of the wits, in which the stronger witted are as sure to succeed as the stronger armed in a war with swords. Strength of wit has this great advantage over strength of arm, that it never tires, for it gathers new strength by appropriating to itself the spoils of the vanquished. And thus, whether between nations or individuals, the war of free trade is constantly widening the relative abilities of the weak and the strong. It has been justly observed that under this system the rich are continually growing richer and the poor poorer. The remark is true as well between nations as between individuals. Free trade, when the American gives a bottle of whiskey to the Indian for valuable furs, or the Englishman exchanges with the African

blue-beads for diamonds, gold and slaves, is a
fair specimen of all free trade when unequals
meet. Free trade between England and Ireland
furnishes the latter an excellent market for her
beef and potatoes, in exchange for English manufactures. The labor employed in manufacturing
pays much better than that engaged in rearing
beeves and potatoes. On the average, one hour
of English labor pays for two of Irish. Again,
manufacturing requires and encourages skill and
intelligence; grazing and farming require none.
But far the worst evils of this free trade remain
to be told. Irish pursuits depressing education
and refinement, England becomes a market for
the wealth, the intellect, the talent, energy and
enterprise of Ireland. All men possessing any of
these advantages or qualities retreat to England
to spend their incomes, to enter the church, the
navy, or the army, to distinguish themselves as
authors, to engage in mechanic or manufacturing
pursuits. Thus is Ireland robbed of her very
life's blood, and thus do our Northern States rob
the Southern.

Under the system of free trade a fertile soil,
with good rivers and roads as outlets, becomes
the greatest evil with which a country can be
afflicted. The richness of soil invites to agricul-
culture, and the roads and rivers carry off the
crops, to be exchanged for the manufactures of

poorer regions, where are situated the centres of trade, of capital and manufactures. In a few centuries or less time the consumption abroad of the crops impoverishes the soil where they are made. No cities or manufactories arise in the country with this fertile soil, because there is no occasion. No pursuits are carried on requiring intelligence or skill; the population is of necessity sparse, ignorant and illiterate; universal absenteeism prevails; the rich go off for pleasure and education, the enterprising poor for employment. An intelligent friend suggests that, left to nature, the evil will cure itself. So it may when the country is ruined, if the people, like those of Georgia, are of high character, and betake themselves to other pursuits than mere agriculture, and totally repudiate free trade doctrines. Our friends' objection only proves the truth of our theory. We are very sure that the wit of man can devise no means so effectual to impoverish a country as exclusive agriculture. The ravages of war, pestilence and famine are soon effaced; centuries are required to restore an exhausted soil. The more rapidly money is made in such a country, enjoying free trade, the faster it is impoverished, for the draft on the soil is greater, and those who make good crops spend them abroad; those who make small ones, at home. In the absence of free trade, this rich region must manufacture for itself, build cities, erect schools and colleges, and carry on all the pursuits and provide for all the common wants of civilized man. Thus the money made at home would be spent and invested at home; the crops would be consumed at home, and each town and village would furnish manure to fertilize the soil around it. We believe it is a common theory that, without this domestic consumption, no soil can be kept permanently rich. A dense population would arise, because it would be required; the rich would have no further occasion to leave home for pleasure, nor the poor for employment.

The valley of the Great Salt Lake is cut off by mountains from the rest of the world, except for travel. Suppose it to continue so cut off, and to be settled by a virtuous, enlightened people. Every trade, every art, every science, must be taught and practiced within a small compass and by a small population, in order to gratify their wants and their tastes. The highest, most diffused and intense civilization, with great accumulation of wealth, would be the necessary result. But let a river like the Mississippi pass through it. Let its inhabitants become merely agricultural, and exchange their products for the manufactures of Europe and the fruits of Asia, and would not that civilization soon disappear, and with it the wealth and capital of the country? Mere agriculture requires no skill or education, few and cheap houses, and no permanent outlay of capital in the construction of the thousand edifices needed in a manufacturing country. Besides, the consumption of the crops abroad would be cheating their lands of that manure which nature intended for them. Soon the rich and enlightened, who owned property there, would, like Irish landlords, live and spend their incomes elsewhere.

The profits of exclusive agriculture are not more than one-third of those realized from commerce and manufactures. The ordinary and average wages of laborers employed in manufactures and mechanic trades are about double those of agricultural laborers; but, moreover, women and children get good wages in manufacturing countries, whose labor is lost in agricultural ones. But this consideration, great as it is, shrinks to insignificance compared with the intellectual superiority of all other pursuits over agriculture.

The centralizing effects of free trade alone would be sufficient to condemn it. The decline of civilization under the Roman Empire was owing solely to centralization. If political science has at all advanced since the earliest annals of history, that advance is the discovery that each small section knows best its own interests, and should be endowed with the most of the functions of government. The ancients, in the days of Herodotus, when the country around the Levant and the Islands in the Mediterranean were cut up into hundreds of little highly enlightened independent States, seem to have understood the evils of centralization quite as well as the moderns. At least their practice was wiser than ours, whatever may have been their theory. Political independence is not worth a fig without commercial independence. The tribute which the centres of trade, of capital, and of mechanical and artistic skill, such as England and the North exact from the nations they trade with, is more onerous and more destructive of civilization than that exacted from conquered provinces. Its effects everywhere are too obvious to need the citation of proofs and instances. Social centralization arises from the *laissez-faire* system just as national centralization. A few individuals possessed of capital and cunning acquire a power to employ the laboring class on such terms as they please, and they seldom fail to use that power. Hence, the numbers and destitution of the poor in free society are daily increasing, the numbers of the middle or independent class diminishing, and the few rich men growing hourly richer.

Free trade occasions a vast and useless, probably a very noxious waste of capital and labor, in exchanging the productions of different and distant climes and regions. Furs and oils are not needed at the South, and the fruits of the tropics are tasteless and insipid at the North. Providence has wonderfully adapted the productions of each section to the wants of man and other animals inhabiting those sections. It is probable, if the subject were scientifically investigated, it would be found that the productions of one clime when used in another are injurious and deleterious. The intercourse of travel and the interchange of ideas it occasions advances civilization. The intercourse of trade, by accustoming barbarous, savage and agricultural countries to depend daily more and more on the centres of trade and manufactures for their supplies of every thing requiring skill or science for its production, rapidly depresses civilization. On the whole subject of civilization there is a prevalent error. Man's necessities civilize him, or rather the labor, invention and ingenuity needed to supply them. Relieve him of the necessity to exert those qualities by supplying through trade or other means his wants, and he at once begins to sink into barbarism. Wars are fine civilizers, for all men dread violent death; hence, among barbarians, the implements of warfare are far superior to any other of their manufactures, but they lead the way to other improvements. The

old adage, that " necessity is the mother of invention," contains our theory; for invention alone
begets civilization. Civilization is no foreign hot-
bed exotic brought from distant climes, but a
hardy plant of indigenous birth and growth.
There never was yet found a nation of white
savages; their wants and their wits combine to
elevate them above the savage state. Nature,
that imposed more wants on them, has kindly
endowed them with superior intelligence to supply those wants.

Political economy is quite as objectionable,
viewed as a rule of morals, as when viewed as a
system of economy. Its authors never seem to
be aware that they are writing an ethical as well
as an economical code; yet it is probable that
no writings, since the promulgation of the Christian dispensation, have exercised so controlling
an influence on human conduct as the writings
of these authors. The morality which they teach
is one of simple and unadulterated selfishness.
The public good, the welfare of society, the prosperity of one's neighbors, is, according to them,
best promoted by each man's looking solely to the
advancement of his own pecuniary interests.
They maintain that national wealth, happiness
and prosperity being but the aggregate of individual wealth, happiness and prosperity, if each
man pursues exclusively his own selfish good, he

is doing the most he can to promote the general good. They seem to forget that men eager in the pursuit of wealth are never satisfied with the fair earnings of their own bodily labor, but find their wits and cunning employed in over-reaching others much more profitable than their hands. *Laissez-faire*, free competition begets a war of the wits, which these economists encourage, quite as destructive to the weak, simple and guileless, as the war of the sword.

In a book on society, evincing much power and originality of thought, by Stephen Pearl Andrews, this subject is well handled. We annex a short extract: "It follows, from what has been said, that the value principle is the commercial embodiment of the essential element of conquest and war—war transferred from the battle-field to the counter—none the less opposed, however, to the spirit of christian morality, or the sentiment of human brotherhood. In bodily conflict, the physically strong conquer and subject the physically weak. In the conflict of trade, the intellectually astute and powerful conquer and subject those who are intellectually feeble, or whose intellectual development is not of the precise kind to fit them for the conflict of wits in the matter of trade. With the progress of civilization and development, we have ceased to think that superior strength gives the *right* of

conquest and subjugation. We have graduated
in idea out of the period of physical dominion.
We remain, however, as yet, in the period of
intellectual conquest or plunder. It has not been
questioned hitherto, as a general proposition, that
the man who has superior intellectual endow-
ments to others, has a right resulting therefrom
to profit thereby at the cost of others. In the
extreme applications of the admission only is the
conclusion denied. (That is, as he had before
said, 'You must not be too bad.' 'Don't gouge
too deep.') In the whole field of what are de-
nominated the legitimate operations of trade,
there is no other law recognized than the relative 'smartness' or shrewdness of the parties,
modified at most by the sentimental precept stated above."

It begets another war in the bosom of society
still more terrible than this. It arrays capital
against labor. Every man is taught by political
economy that it is meritorious to make the best
bargains one can. In all old countries, labor is
superabundant, employers less numerous than laborers; yet all the laborers must live by the
wages they receive from the capitalists. The
capitalist cheapens their wages; they compete
with and underbid each other, for employed they
must be on any terms. This war of the rich
with the poor and the poor with one another, is

the morality which political economy inculcates.
It is the only morality, save the Bible, recognized or acknowledged in free society, and is far
more efficacious in directing worldly men's conduct than the Bible, for that teaches self-denial,
not self-indulgence and aggrandizement. This
process of underbidding each other by the poor,
which universal liberty necessarily brings about,
has well been compared by the author of Alton
Locke to the prisoners in the Black Hole of
Calcutta strangling one another. A beautiful
system of ethics this, that places all mankind
in antagonistic positions, and puts all society at
war. What can such a war result in but the oppression and ultimate extermination of the weak?
In such society the astute capitalist, who is very
skilful and cunning, gets the advantage of every
one with whom he competes or deals; the sensible man with moderate means gets the advantage of most with whom he has business, but
the mass of the simple and poor are outwitted
and cheated by everybody.

Woman fares worst when thrown into this warfare of competition. The delicacy of her sex
and her nature prevents her exercising those
coarse arts which men do in the vulgar and pro-
miscuous jostle of life, and she is reduced to the
necessity of getting less than half price for her
work. To the eternal disgrace of human nature,

the men who employ her value themselves on the
Adam Smith principle for their virtuous and sensible conduct. "Labor is worth what it will
bring; they have given the poor woman more
than any one else would, or she would not have
taken the work." Yet she and her children are
starving, and the employer is growing rich by
giving her half what her work is worth. Thus
does free competition, the creature of free society, throw the whole burden of the social fabric
on the poor, the weak and ignorant. They produce every thing and enjoy nothing. They are
"the muzzled ox that treadeth out the straw."

In free society none but the selfish virtues are
in repute, because none other help a man in the
race of competition. In such society virtue loses
all her loveliness, because of her selfish aims.
Good men and bad men have the same end in view:
self-promotion, self-elevation. The good man is
prudent, cautious, and cunning of fence; he knows
well, the arts (the virtues, if you please) which
enable him to advance his fortunes at the expense of those with whom he deals; he does not
"cut too deep"; he does not cheat and swindle,
he only makes good bargains and excellent profits.
He gets more subjects by this course; everybody
comes to him to be bled. He bides his time;
takes advantage of the follies, the improvidence
and vices of others, and makes his fortune out

of the follies and weaknesses of his fellow-men. The bad man is rash, hasty, unskilful and impolitic. He is equally selfish, but not half so prudent and cunning. Selfishness is almost the only motive of human conduct in free society, where every man is taught that it is his first duty to change and better his pecuniary situation.

The first principles of the science of political economy inculcate separate, individual action, and are calculated to prevent that association of labor without which nothing great can be achieved; for man isolated and individualized is the most helpless of animals. We think this error of the economists proceeded from their adopting Locke's theory of the social contract. We believe no heresy in moral science has been more pregnant of mischief than this theory of Locke. It lies at the bottom of all moral speculations, and if false, must infect with falsehood all theories built on it. Some animals are by nature gregarious and associative. Of this class are men, ants and bees. An isolated man is almost as helpless and ridiculous as a bee setting up for himself. Man is born a member of society, and does not form society. Nature, as in the cases of bees and ants, has it ready formed for him. He and society are congenital. Society is the being—he one of the members of that being. He has no rights whatever, as opposed to the interests of society;

B

and that society may very properly make any
use of him that will redound to the public good.
Whatever rights he has are subordinate to the
good of the whole; and he has never ceded rights
to it, for he was born its slave, and had no rights
to cede.

Government is the creature of society, and may
be said to derive its powers from the consent of
the governed; but society does not owe its sove-
reign power to the separate consent, volition or
agreement of its members. Like the hive, it is
as much the work of nature as the individuals
who compose it. Consequences, the very opposite
of the doctrine of free trade, result from this doctrine of ours. It makes each society a band of
brothers, working for the common good, instead
of a bag of cats biting and worrying each other.
The competitive system is a system of antagonism
and war; ours of peace and fraternity. The first
is the system of free society; the other that of
slave society. The Greek, the Roman, Judaistic,
Egyptian, and all ancient polities, were founded
on our theory. The loftiest patrician in those
days, valued himself not on selfish, cold individuality, but on being the most devoted servant of
society and his country. In ancient times, the
individual was considered nothing, the State every
thing. And yet, under this system, the noblest
individuality was evolved that the world has ever

seen. The prevalence of the doctrines of political economy has injured Southern character, for in the South those doctrines most prevail. Wealthy men, who are patterns of virtue in the discharge of their domestic duties, value themselves on never intermeddling in public matters. They. forget that property is a mere creature of law and society, and are willing to make no return for that property to the public, which by its laws gave it to them, and which guard and protect them in its possession.

All great enterprises owe their success to association of capital and labor. The North is indebted for its great wealth and prosperity to the readiness with which it forms associations for all industrial and commercial purposes. The success of Southern farming is a striking instance of the value of the association of capital and laborers, and ought to suggest to the South the necessity of it for other purposes.

The dissociation of labor and disintegration of society, which liberty and free competition occasion, is especially injurious to the poorer class; for besides the labor necessary to support the family, the poor man is burdened with the care of finding a home, and procuring employment, and attending to all domestic wants and concerns. Slavery relieves our slaves of these cares altogether, and slavery is a form, and the very best

form, of socialism. In fact, the ordinary wages
of common labor are insufficient to keep up separate domestic establishments for each of the poor,
and association or starvation is in many cases
inevitable. In free society, as well in Europe
as in America, this is the accepted theory, and
various schemes have been resorted to, all without
success, to cure the evil. The association of labor
properly carried out under a common head or
ruler, would render labor more efficient, relieve
the laborer of many of the cares of household
affairs, and protect and support him in sickness
and old age, besides preventing the too great
reduction of wages by redundancy of labor and
free competition. Slavery attains all these results.
What else will?

We find in the days of Sir Matthew Hale, a
very singular pamphlet attributed to him. It was
an attempt to prove that two healthy laborers,
marrying and having in the usual time four children, could not at ordinary labor, and with ordinary wages, support their family. The nursing,
washing, cooking and making clothes, would fully
occupy the wife. The husband, with the chances
of sickness and uncertainty of employment, would
have to support four. Such is the usual and
normal condition of free laborers. With six children, the oldest say twelve years of age, their
condition would be worse. Or should the husband

die, the family that remained would be still worse off. There are large numbers of aged and infirm male and female laborers; so that as a class, it is obvious, we think, that under ordinary circumstances, in old countries, they are incapable of procuring a decent and comfortable support. The wages of the poor diminish as their wants and families increase, for the care and labor of attending to the family leaves them fewer hours for profitable work. With negro slaves, their wages invariably increase with their wants. The master increases the provision for the family as the family increases in number and helplessness. It is a beautiful example of communism, where each one receives not according to his labor, but according to his wants.

A maxim well calculated not only to retard the progress of civilization, but to occasion its retrogression, has grown out of the science of political economy. "The world is too much governed," has become quite an axiom with many politicians. Now the need of law and government is just in proportion to man's wealth and enlightenment. Barbarians and savages need and will submit to but few and simple laws, and little of government. The love of personal liberty and freedom from all restraint, are distinguishing traits of wild men and wild beasts. Our Anglo-Saxon ancestors loved personal liberty because they were barbarians, but they did not love it half so much as North American Indians or Bengal tigers, because they were not half so savage. As civilization advances, liberty recedes : and it is fortunate for man that he loses his love of liberty just as fast as he becomes more moral and intellectual. ˙ The wealthy, virtuous and religious citizens of large towns enjoy less of liberty than any other persons whatever, and yet they are the most useful and rationally happy of all mankind. The best governed countries, and those which have prospered most, have always been distinguished for the number and stringency of their laws. Good men obey superior authority, the laws of God, of morality, and of their country ; bad men love liberty and violate them. It would be difficult very often for the most ingenious casuist to distinguish between sin and liberty ; for virtue consists in the performance of duty, and the obedience to that law or power that imposes duty, whilst sin is but the violation of duty and disobedience to such law and power. It is remarkable, in this connection, that sin began by the desire for liberty and the attempt to attain it in the person of Satan and his fallen angels. The world wants good government and a plenty of it—not liberty. It is deceptive in us to boast of our Democracy, to assert the capacity of the people for self-government, and then refuse to them its exercise. ˙ In

New England, and in all our large cities, where the people govern most, they are governed best. If government be not too much centralized, there is little danger of too much government. The danger and evil with us is of too little. Carlyle says of our institutions, that they are "anarchy plus a street constable." We ought not to be bandaged up too closely in our infancy, it might prevent growth and development; but the time is coming when we shall need more of government, if we would secure the permanency of our institutions.

All men concur in the opinion that some government is necessary. Even the political economist would punish murder, theft, robbery, gross swindling, &c.; but they encourage men to compete with and slowly undermine and destroy one another by means quite as effective as those they forbid. We have heard a distinguished member of this school object to negro slavery, because the protection it afforded to an inferior race would perpetuate that race, which, if left free to compete with the whites, must be starved out in a few generations. Members of Congress, of the Young American party, boast that the Anglo-Saxon race is manifestly destined to eat out all other races, as the wire-grass destroys and takes the place of other grasses. Nay, they allege this competitive process is going on throughout all nature; the weak are everywhere devouring the strong; the hardier plants and animals destroying the weaker, and the superior races of man exterminating the inferior. They would challenge our admiration for this war of nature, by which they say Providence is perfecting its own work—getting rid of what is weak and indifferent, and preserving only what is strong and hardy. We see the war, but not the improvement. This competitive, destructive system has been going on from the earliest records of history; and yet the plants, the animals, and the men of to-day are not superior to those of four thousand years ago. To restrict this destructive, competitive propensity, man was endowed with reason, and enabled to pass laws to protect the weak against the strong. To encourage it, is to encourage the strong to oppress the weak, and to violate the primary object of all government. It is strange it should have entered the head of any philosopher to set the weak, who are the majority of mankind, to competing, contending and fighting with the strong, in order to improve their condition.

Hobbes maintains that "a state of nature is a state of war." This is untrue of a state of nature, because men are naturally associative; but it is true of a civilized state of universal liberty, and free competition, such as Hobbes saw around him, and which no doubt suggested his theory. The wants of man and his history alike prove that slavery has always been part of his social organization. A less degree of subjection is inadequate for the government and protection of great numbers of human beings.

An intelligent English writer, describing society as he saw it, uses this language :

"There is no disguising from the cool eye of philosophy, that all living creatures exist in a state of natural warfare ; and that man (in hostility with all) is at enmity also with his own species ; man is the natural enemy of man ; and society, unable to change his nature, succeeds but in establishing a hollow truce by which fraud is substituted for violence."

Such is free society, fairly portrayed ; such are the infidel doctrines of political economy, when candidly avowed. Slavery and Christianity bring about a lasting peace, not "a hollow truce." But we mount a step higher. We deny that there is a society in free countries. They who act each for himself, who are hostile, antagonistic and competitive, are not social and do not constitute a society. We use the term free society, for want of a better ; but, like the term free government, it is an absurdity : those who are governed are not free—those who are free are not social.

CHAPTER II.

The phenomena presented by the vassals and villiens of Europe after their liberation, were the opposite of those exhibited by the wealthy and powerful classes. Pauperism and beggary, we are informed by English historians, were unknown till the villiens began to escape from their masters, and attempted to practise a predatory and nomadic liberty. A liberty, we should infer from the descriptions we can get of it, very much like that of domestic animals that have gone wild— the difference in favor of the animals being that nature had made provision for them, but had made none for the villiens. The new freemen were bands of thieves and beggars, infesting the country and disturbing its peace. Their physical condition was worse than when under the rule of the Barons, their masters, and their moral condition worse also, for liberty had made them from necessity thieves and murderers. It was necessary to retain them in slavery, not only to support and sustain them and to prevent general mendicity, but equally necessary in order to govern them and prevent crime. The advocates of universal liberty concede that the laboring class enjoy more material comfort, are better fed, clothed and housed, as slaves, than as freemen. The statistics of crime demonstrate that the moral superiority of the slave over the free laborer is still greater than his superiority in animal well-being. There never can be among slaves a class so degraded as is found about the wharves and suburbs of cities. The master requires and enforces ordinary morality and industry. We very much fear, if it were possible to indite a faithful comparison of the conduct and comfort of our free negroes with that of the runaway Anglo-Saxon serfs, that it would be found that the negroes have fared better and committed much less crime than the whites. But those days, the 14th and 15th centuries, were the halcyon days of vagabond liberty. The few that had escaped from bondage found a wide field and plenty of subjects for the practice of theft and mendicity. There was no law and no police adequate to restrain them, for until then their masters had kept them in order better than laws ever can. But those glorious old times have long since passed. A bloody code, a standing army and efficient police keep them quiet enough now. Their numbers have multiplied a hundred fold, but their poverty has increased faster than their numbers. Instead of stealing and begging, and living idly in the open air, they work fourteen hours a day, cooped up in close rooms, with foul air, foul water, and insufficient and filthy food, and often sleep at night crowded in cellars or in garrets, without regard to sex.

In proceeding to prove that this is a correct account of the effects in England of liberating the laboring class, we are at much difficulty how to select from the mass of testimony that at every turn presents itself to us. We are not aware that any one disputes the fact that crime and pauperism throughout Western Europe increased *pari passu* with liberty, equality and free competition. We know of but a single respectable authority that disputes the fact that this increase is directly attributable to free competition or liberty. Even the Edinburgh Review, hitherto the great champion of political economy and free competition, has been silent on the subject for several years. With strange inconsistency, the very men who assert that universal liberty has, and must ever, from the nature of things, increase crime, mendicity and pauperism among the laboring class, maintain that slavery degrades this very class whom it preserves from poverty and crime. The elevation of the scaffold is the only moral or physical elevation that they can point to which distinguishes the condition of the free laborer from his servile ancestor. The peasantry of England,

in the days of Cressey, Agincourt and Shrews-
bury, when feudalism prevailed, were generally
brave, virtuous, and in the enjoyment of a high
degree of physical comfort—at least, that comfort differed very little from that of their lords
and masters. This same peasantry, when Charles
Edward with three thousand Highlanders invaded
England, had become freemen and cowards. Starving Frenchmen will at least fight, but starving
Chartists only bluster. How slavery could degrade men lower than universal liberty has done,
it is hard to conceive; how it did and would
again preserve them from such degradation, is well
explained by those who are loudest in its abuse.
A consciousness of security, a full comprehension of his position, and a confidence in that position, and the absence of all corroding cares and
anxieties, makes the slave easy and self-assured
in his address, cheerful, happy and contented,
free from jealousy, malignity, and envy, and at
peace with all around him. His attachment to
his master begets the sentiment of loyalty, than
which none more purifies and elevates human nature. This theory of the moral influences of
slavery is suggested and in part borrowed from
Alexandre Dumas' "French Milliner." He, descended from a negro slave, and we may presume prejudiced against slavery, speaks in glow-
ing terms of its happy influence on the lives and

manners of the Russian serfs. He draws a contrast between their cheerfulness and the wretch-
edness of the French laboring class, and attributes solely to the feeling of security which
slavery induces, their enviable cheerfulness.

The free laborer rarely has a house and home
of his own; he is insecure of employment; sickness may overtake him at any time and deprive
him of the means of support; old age is certain
to overtake him, if he lives, and generally finds
him without the means of subsistence; his family
is probably increasing in numbers, and is helpless and burdensome to him. In all this there
is little to incite to virtue, much to tempt to
crime, nothing to afford happiness, but quite
enough to inflict misery. Man must be more
than human, to acquire a pure and a high morality under such circumstances.

In free society the sentiments, principles, feelings and affections of high and low, rich and
poor, are equally blunted and debased by the
continual war of competition. It begets rivalries, jealousies and hatreds on all hands. The
poor can neither love nor respect the rich, who,
instead of aiding and protecting them, are endeavoring to cheapen their labor and take away
their means of subsistence. The rich can hardly
respect themselves, when they reflect that wealth
is the result of avarice, caution, circumspection

and hard dealing. These are the virtues which
free society in its regular operation brings forth.
Its moral influence is therefore no better on the
rich than on the poor. The number of laborers
being excessive in all old countries, they are continually struggling with, scandalizing and underbidding each other, to get places and employment. Every circumstance in the poor man's situation in free society is one of harassing care,
of grievous temptation, and of excitement to an-
ger, envy, jealousy and malignity. That so many
of the poor should nevertheless be good and pure,
kind, happy and high-minded, is proof enough
that the poor class is not the worst class in society. But the rich have their temptations, too.
Capital gives them the power to oppress; selfishness offers the inducement, and political economy,
the moral guide of the day, would justify the
oppression. Yet there are thousands of noble
and generous and disinterested men in free society, who employ their wealth to relieve, and not
to oppress the poor. Still these are exceptions
to the general rule. The effect of such society
is to encourage the oppression of the poor.

The ink was hardly dry with which Adam Smith
wrote his Wealth of Nations, lauding the benign
influences of free society, ere the hunger and
want and nakedness of that society engendered a
revolutionary explosion that shook the world to

its centre. The starving artisans and laborers, and fish-women and needle-women of Paris, were the authors of the first French revolution, and that revolution was everywhere welcomed, and spread from nation to nation like fire in the prairies. The French armies met with but a formal opposition, until they reached Russia. There, men had homes and houses and a country to fight for. The serfs of Russia, the undisciplined Cossacks, fought for lares and penates, their homes, their country, and their God, and annihilated an army more numerous than that of Xerxes, and braver and better appointed than the tenth legion of Cæsar. What should Western European poor men fight for? All the world was the same to them. They had been set free to starve, without a place to rest their dying heads or to inter their dead bodies. Any change they thought would be for the better, and hailed Buonaparte as a deliverer. But the nature of the evil was not understood; there were some remnants of feudalism, some vigor in the Catholic church; these Buonaparte swept away, and left the poor without a stay or a hope. Buonaparte is conquered and banished, universal peace restored; commerce, mechanic arts, manufactures and agriculture revive and flourish; invention is stimulated, industry urged on to its utmost exertion. Never seemed the world so prosperous, so happy, so

progressive. But only seemed! Those awful statistics unfold the sad tale that misery and crime
and poverty are on the increase still. The pris-
ons are filled, the poor houses and the penal
colonies supplied too fast, and the gallows ever
pendant with its subject. In 1830, Paris starves
again, builds barricades, continues hungry, and
hesitates what next to do. Finally sets up a
new king, no better than the one she has expelled. Revolution follows revolution with electric speed throughout great part of Western Europe. Kings are deposed, governments changed;
soon new kings put in their places, and things
subside—not quietly—into the *status quo ante
bellum*. All this, while millions of the poor are
fleeing from Europe as men fly from an infected
plague spot, to seek their fortunes in other climes
and regions. Another eighteen years of hunger,
of crime, of riots, strikes, and trades unions,
passes over free society. In 1848 the drama of
1830 is almost literally re-enacted. Again Paris
starves, builds barricades, and expels her king.
Again Western Europe follows her example. By
this time, however, men had discovered that political changes would not cure the diseases of
society. The poor must have bread; government
must furnish it. Liberty without bread was not
worth fighting for. A Republic is set up in
Paris that promises employment and good wages

to every body. The experiment is tried and fails
in a week. No employment, except transplanting trees and levelling mounds, could be found,
and the treasury breaks. After struggling and
blundering and staggering on through various
changes, Louis Napoleon is made Emperor. He
is a socialist, and socialism is the new fashion-
able name of slavery. He understands the disease of society, and has nerve enough for any
surgical operation that may be required to cure
it. His first step in socialism was to take the
money of the rich to buy wheat for all. The
measure was well-timed, necessary and just. He
is now building houses on the social plan for
working men, and his Queen is providing nurse-
ries and nurses for the children of the working
women, just as we Southerners do for our negro
women and children. It is a great economy.
Fourier suggested it long after Southerners had
practiced it. During these times there was a
little episode in Ireland—Ireland, the freest country in the world, where law is violated every
day, mocked at and derided, whence the rich
and the noble have emigrated, where all are poor,
all equal, and all idle. A few thousands only
had usually starved annually; but the potatoe
crop failed; they had no feudal lords to buy
other food for them, and three hundred thousand starved in a single season. No slave or

serf ever did starve, unless he were a runaway. Irishmen, although they love liberty to distraction, have lost their taste for starving. They are coming *en masse* to America, and in a few years, at the present rate of emigration, will leave the island without inhabitants. The great and increasing emigration from free society in Europe can only be accounted for on the ground that they believe their social system so rotten that no mere political change can help them—for a political revolution can be had on twenty-four hours' notice.

The Chartists and Radicals of England would in some way subvert and re-construct society. They complain of free competition as a crying evil, and may be classed with the Socialists. The high conservative party called Young England vainly endeavors, by preaching fine sentiments, to produce that good feeling between the rich and the poor, the weak and the powerful, which slavery alone can bring about. Liberty places those classes in positions of antagonism and war. Slavery identifies the interests of rich and poor, master and slave, and begets domestic affection on the one side, and loyalty and respect on the other. Young England sees clearly enough the character of the disease, but is not bold enough to propose an adequate remedy. The poor themselves are all practical Socialists, and in some degree pro-slavery men. They unite in strikes and trades unions, and thus exchange a part of their liberties in order to secure high and uniform wages. The exchange is a prudent and sensible one; but they who have bartered off liberty, are fast verging towards slavery. Slavery to an association is not always better than slavery to a single master. The professed object is to avoid ruinous under-bidding and competition with one another; but this competition can never cease whilst liberty lasts. Those who wish to be free must take liberty with this inseparable burden. Odd-Fellows' societies, temperance societies, and all other societies that provide for sick and unfortunate members, are instances of Socialism. The muse in England for many years has been busy in composing dissonant laborer songs, bewailing the hardships, penury and sufferings of the poor, and indignantly rebuking the cruelty and injustice of their hard-hearted and close-fisted employers.

Dickens and Bulwer denounce the frame-work of society quite as loudly as Carlyle and Newman; the two latter of whom propose slavery as a remedy for existing evils. A large portion of the clergy are professed Socialists, and there is scarcely a literary man in England who is not ready to propose radical and organic changes in her social system. Germany is full of Communists; social discontent is universal, and her people are leaving *en masse* for America—hopeless of any amelioration at home for the future. Strange to tell, in the free States of America too, Socialism and every other heresy that can be invoked to make war on existing institutions, prevail to an alarming extent. Even according to our own theory of the necessity of slavery, we should not suppose that that necessity would be so soon felt in a new and sparsely-settled country, where the supply of labor does not exceed the demand. But it is probable the constant arrival of emigrants makes the situation of the laborer at the North as precarious as in Europe, and produces a desire for some change that shall secure him employment and support at all times. Slavery alone can effect that change; and towards slavery the North and all Western Europe are unconsciously marching. The master evil they all complain of is free competition—which is another name for liberty. Let them remove that evil, and they will find themselves slaves, with all the advantages and disadvantages of slavery. They will have attained association of labor, for slavery produces association of labor, and is one of the ends all Communists and Socialists desire. A well-conducted farm in the South is a model of associated labor that Fourier might envy. One old woman nurses all the children whilst the mothers are at work; another waits on the sick, in a house set aside for them. Another washes and cooks, and a fourth makes and mends the clothing. It is a great economy of labor, and is a good idea of the Socialists. Slavery protects the infants, the aged and the sick; nay, takes far better care of them than of the healthy, the middle-aged and the strong. They are part of the family, and self-interest and domestic affection combine to shelter, shield and foster them. A man loves not only his horses and his cattle, which are useful to him, but he loves his dog, which is of no use. He loves them because they are his. What a wise and beneficent provision of Heaven, that makes the selfishness of man's nature a protecting ægis to shield and defend wife and children, slaves and even dumb animals. The Socialists propose to reach this result too, but they never can if they refuse to march in the only road Providence has pointed out. Who will check, govern and control their superintending authority? Who prevent his abuse of power? Who can make him kind, tender and affectionate, to the poor, aged, helpless, sick and unfortunate? *Qui custodiat custodes?* Nature establishes the only safe and reliable checks and balances in government. Alton Locke describes an English farm, where the cattle, the horses and the sheep are fat, plentifully fed and warmly housed; the game in the preserves and the fish in the pond carefully provided for; and two freezing, shivering, starving, half-clad boys, who have to work on the Sabbath, are the slaves to these animals, and are vainly endeavoring to prepare their food. Now it must have occurred to the author that if the boys had belonged to the owner of the farm, they too would have been well-treated, happy and contented. This farm is but a miniature of all England; every animal is well-treated and provided for, except the laboring man. He is the slave of the brutes, the slave of society, produces everything and enjoys nothing. Make him the slave of one man, instead of the slave of society, and he would be far better off. None but lawyers and historians are aware how much of truth, justice and good sense, there is in the notions of the Communists, as to the community of property. Laying no stress on the too abstract proposition that Providence gave the world not to one man, or set of men, but to all mankind, it is a fact that all governments, in civilized countries, recognize the obligation to support the poor, and thus, in some degree, make all property a common possession. The poor laws and poor houses of England are founded on communistic principles. Each parish is compelled to support its own poor. In Ireland, this obligation weighs so heavily as in many instances to make farms valueless; the poor rates exceeding the rents. But it is domestic slavery alone that can establish a safe, efficient and humane community of property. It did so in ancient times, it did so in feudal times, and does so now, in Eastern Europe, Asia and America. Slaves never die of hunger; seldom suffer want. Hence Chinese sell themselves when they can do no better. A Southern farm is a sort of joint stock concern, or social phalastery, in which the master furnishes the capital and skill, and the slaves the labor, and divide the profits, not according to each one's in-put, but according to each one's wants and necessities.

Socialism proposes to do away with free competition; to afford protection and support at all times to the laboring class; to bring about, at least, a qualified community of property, and to associate labor. All these purposes, slavery fully and perfectly attains.

To prove the evil effects, moral, social and economic, of the emancipation of feudal slaves or villiens, and how those evil effects gave birth to Socialism, we quote first from the Pictorial History of England:

"To the period (15th century,) immediately preceding the present, belongs the origin of English pauperism, as well as of the legislation on the subject of the poor. So long as the system of villienage was maintained in its integrity, there could be no paupers in the land; that is to say, no persons left destitute of the means of subsistence, except beggary or public alms. The principle of that institution was, that every individual who had nothing else, had at least a right of food and shelter from the landed proprietor whose bondsman he was. The master was not more entitled to the services of his villien, than the villien was to the maintenance of himself and his family, at the expense of his master. This has of absolute necessity been the law in every country in which slavery has existed. * * * * But as soon as the original slavery of the English laboring population begun to be exchanged for freedom, and villienage gradually, and at last generally passed away in the manner stated in the last book, the working man, now his own master, was of course left in all circumstances to his own resources; and when either want of employment, or sickness, or the helplessness of old age came upon him, if he had not saved something from his former earnings, and had no one to take care of him from motives of affection or compassion, his condition was as unprovided for as that of the fowls of the heavens. But men will not starve, whilst they can either beg or steal; hence, the first appearance that the destitute poor, as a class of the community, make in our annals, is in the character of *thieves* and mendicants, sometimes enforcing their demands by threats or violence."— Vol. 2d, pages 262, 263.

c

Such is the description of free society at its birth, by authors who hate and denounce slavery. We will proceed to prove from like authority, that the number of mendicants and thieves has increased with accelerating speed from that day to this.

We find in Hume's History of England, treating of the discontents of the people in the reign of Edward VI., the following language :

"There is no abuse in civil society so great as not to be attended with a variety of beneficial consequences ; and in the beginnings of reformation, the loss of these advantages is always felt very sensibly, while the benefit resulting from the change is the slow effect of time, and is seldom perceived by the bulk of the nation. Scarce any institution can be imagined less favorable in the main to the interests of mankind, than that of monks and friars ; yet was it followed by many good effects, which having ceased by the suppression of the monasteries, were much regretted by the people of England. The monks always residing in their convents in the centre of their estates, spent their money in the provinces, and among their tenants, afforded a ready market for commodities, and were a sure resource to the poor and indigent ; and though their hospitality and charity gave too much encouragement to idleness, and prevented the increase of public riches, yet did it provide to many a relief from the extreme pressure of want and necessity."

In the Pictorial History of England, under the head of the Condition of the People, about the 16th and 17th centuries, we find crime and pauperism still on the increase, and hundreds of essays and books written and many acts of Parliament passed on this perplexing and growing evil in free society. But it was after Napoleon had made a dead level of Western European society, a sort of "*tabula raza*," by destroying the remnants of feudalism and crippling and cramping the Catholic Church, that liberty and free competition were first given free scope and elbow-room. Not till then had the doctrines, that "might makes right" and "every man for himself, and devil take the hindmost," been brought into full play. The natural consequence was, that the strong conquered and devoured the weak much faster than they had ever done before. The world of the political economists, the rich, the astute, the avaricious, the prudent, the circumspect and hard-hearted, started forward with railroad speed and railroad recklessness. The world of the Socialists, (vastly increased in numbers,) the poor, the weak, ignorant, generous and improvident, ran backwards quite as fast as the other world went forward. Almost every middle-aged man who can read a newspaper, is aware, that whilst the aggregate wealth of civilized mankind has increased more rapidly since the fall of Napoleon than it ever did before, and whilst the discoveries and inventions in physical science have rapidly lessened the amount of labor necessary to procure human subsistence and comfort, yet these advantages have been monopolized by the few, and the laboring millions are in worse condition (in free society) than they ever were before. On this subject we shall quote from two able articles in Blackwood, not because our positions need proof, but because these quotations will throw much light on the character of the disease under which free society is suffering, and show that protection of some kind is imperiously demanded to shield the masses from the grinding oppression of universal liberty, free competition and *laissez-faire*, and to show that it is the carrying into practical operation the theories of the political economists, or free trade men, that has occasioned the unexampled progress and prosperity of the few who are strong, and the appalling and increasing crime and destitution of the many, who are weak. Further, these quotations will sustain and illustrate our doctrine that the political economists have taken partial views of society, and have mistaken the good luck and success of their friends for the general condition and fortune of mankind. Blackwood seems to contemplate protection against foreign competition as an adequate remedy. We leave it to the intelligent reader to say, whether protection against social and domestic competition is not quite as necessary—and nothing but slavery can afford this latter protection.

In a review of Alton Locke in Blackwood, Nov. No. 1850, the following passages will be found:

"No man with a human heart in his bosom, unless that heart is utterly indurated and depraved by the influence of mammon, can be indifferent to the fate of the working classes. Even if he were not urged to consider the awful social questions which daily demand our attention in this perplexing and bewildered age, by the impulses of humanity or by the call of Christian duty, the lower motive of interest alone should incline him to serious reflection on a subject which involves the well-being, both temporal and eternal, of thousands of his fellow-beings, and possibly the permanence of order and tranquility in this realm of Great Britain. Our civil history during the last thirty years of peace, resembles nothing which the world has yet seen or which can be found in the records of civilization. The progress which has been made in the mechanical sciences is of itself almost equivalent to a revolution. The whole face of society has been altered; old employments have become obsolete, old customs have been altered or remodelled, and old institutions have

undergone innovation. The modern citizen thinks
and acts differently from his fathers. What to
them was object of reverence, is to him subject
of ridicule; what they were accustomed to prize
and honor, he regards with undisguised contempt.
All this we call improvement, taking no heed
the while whether such improvement has fulfilled
the primary condition of contributing to and increasing the welfare and prosperity of the people.
Statistical books are written to. prove how enor-
mously we have increased in wealth; and yet, side
by side with Mr. Porter's bulky tome, you will
find pamphlets containing ample and distinct evidence that hundreds of thousands of our industrious fellow-countrymen are at this moment fam-
ishing for lack of employment, or compelled to
sell their labor for such wretched compensation,
that the pauper's dole is by many regarded with
absolute envy. Dives and Lazarus elbow one
another in the street, *and our political economists
select Dives as the sole type of the nation.* San-
itary commissioners are appointed to whiten the
outside of the sepulchre; and during the operation
their stomachs are made sick by the taint of the rot-
tenness within. The reform of Parliament is, com-
paratively speaking, a matter of yesterday; and
yet the operatives are petitioning for the charter!
These are stern realities, grave facts, which it
is impossible to gainsay. What may be the re-

sult of them, unless some adequate remedy can be provided, it is impossible with certainty to predict; but unless we are prepared to deny the doctrine of that retribution which has been directly revealed to us from above, and of which the history of neighboring states affords us so many striking examples, we can hardly expect to remain unpunished for what is truly a national crime. The offence, indeed, according to all the elements of human calculation, is likely to bring its own punishment. It cannot be that society can exist in tranquility, or order be permanently maintained, so long as a large portion of the working classes, of the hard-handed men whose industry makes capital move and multiply itself, are exposed to the operation of a system that makes their position less tolerable than that of Egyptian bondsmen. To work is not only a duty, but a privilege; but to work against hope, to toil under the absolute pressure of despair, is the most miserable lot that the imagination can possibly conceive. It is, in fact, a virtual abrogation of that freedom which every Briton is taught to consider his birthright, but which now, however well it may sound as an abstract term, is practically, in the case of thousands, placed utterly beyond their reach.

We shall not probably be suspected of any intention to inculcate radical doctrines. We have no sympathy, but the reverse, with the quacks, visionaries and agitators, who make a livelihood by preaching disaffection in our towns and cities, and who are the worst enemies of the people whose cause they pretend to advocate. We detest the selfish views of the Manchester school of politicians, and we loathe that hypocrisy which, under the pretext of reforming, would destroy the institutions of the country. But, if it be true, as we believe it to be, that the working and producing classes of the community are suffering unexampled hardship, and that not of a temporary and exceptional kind, but from the operation of some vicious and baneful element that has crept into our social system, it then becomes our duty to attempt to discover the actual nature of the evil; and, having discovered that, to consider seriously what cure it is possible to apply." * * * "Here is a question urgently presenting itself to the consideration of all thinking men; a question which concerns the welfare of hundreds of thousands; a question which has been evaded by statesmen so long as they dared to do so with impunity; but which now can be no longer evaded: that question being, whether any possible means can be found for ameliorating and improving the condition of the working classes of Great Britain, by rescuing them *from the cruel effects of that competition which makes each man*

the enemy of his fellow; which is annually dri-
ving from our shores crowds of our best and
most industrious artisans; which consigns women
from absolute indigence to infamy; dries up the
most sacred springs of affection in the heart;
crams the jail and the poor-house; and is eat-
ing like a fatal canker into the very heart-blood
of society." This subject was deemed by Blackwood so important, that it was resumed in a
subsequent number of that review, "The Dan-
gers of the Country," March number, 1851. We
will not fatigue the reader's attention with extracts from that article, which is a most able and
interesting one; but will merely state that, after
giving tedious and careful statistics, showing the
rapid and unexampled increase of crime and pauperism in Great Britain since 1819, a period in
which the prosperity of the upper classes was as
remarkable as the continually increasing debase-
ment and misery of the lower, the Reviewer concludes with these emphatic words: "But this we
do say, and with these words we nail our colors
to the mast, PROTECTION MUST BE RESTORED, OR
THE BRITISH EMPIRE WILL BE DISSOLVED." Now
the evil complained of is free competition, and
nothing short of some modification of slavery can
give protection against free competition. To leave
no room for cavil or doubt as to the truth of
our positions, that pauperism commenced and crime

was increased with the birth of the liberty of the laboring class, and that each extension of liberty has immediately occasioned an accelerated increase of poverty and crime, we wish to adduce authorities, not only of the highest character, but representing all parties and shades of opinion. We now quote from the April number, 1854, of the Westminster Review on "The Results of the Census." After treating of the breaking up of the feudal system and dissolution of the Catholic church, the writer thus proceeds: "These interests having gone down and another class having arisen, is there any other to be considered? Yes, an enormous one—an appalling one—the pauper interest. Long before the dissolution of the monasteries, the pauperism of the country had become an almost unmanageable evil. *It began with the abolition of serfage;* and the monasteries absorbed as much as they could of an existing evil, increasing it all the while. From the fourteenth century there had been laws to restrain vagrancy; and in the sixteenth it had increased 'to the marvellous disturbance of the common weal of this realm.' Beggars went about, 'valiant and sturdy,' in great 'routs and companies.' The vagrants were to be put in prison, branded and whipped; the clergy were to press all good citizens to give alms; and all who were able must find employment for those who could work. Then came the compulsory tax: and then the celebrated 43d Elizabeth; and all apparently in vain. The lower class had not risen, generally speaking, with the middle; and there was as wide an interval between that middle class and the pauper banditti of the realm, as there once was between the landed class and the serfs." Pauper banditti! And this is what two hundred years of liberty makes of white laborers. And now four hundred years have passed over, and their condition is getting daily worse; they are quitting their homes—no, not homes, for they have none—but flying from the land that has persecuted them to every wild and desert corner of the earth.

The cotemporaneous appearance of Alton Locke and a vast number of pamphlets and essays on the subject of the sufferings and crimes of the laboring class in Great Britain, forms a most interesting epoch in the history of social science. No one who pays the least attention to the subject, will doubt that the doctrines and philosophy of socialism or communism, which just then became rife in England, owed their birth to the increased and increasing sufferings of the poor, which that philosophy proposes to remove. The Edinburgh Review, in its January number, 1851, discourses as follows: "As long as socialism was confined to the turbulent, the wild and the disreputable, and was associated with tenets which made it disgusting and disreputable, perhaps the wisest plan was to pass it over in silence, and suffer it to die of its own inherent weakness. But now, when it has appeared in a soberer guise and purified from much of its evil intermixtures; when it has shown itself an actual and energetic reality in France; when it has spread among the intelligent portions of the working classes in our own country more extensively than is commonly believed; when it raises its head under various modifications, and often as it were unconsciously, in the disquisitions which issue from the periodical press; when a weekly journal, conducted with great ability as to every thing but logic, is devoted to its propagation; and when clergymen of high literary reputation give in their scarcely qualified adherence, and are actively engaged in reducing to practice their own peculiar modification of the theory, it would be no longer kindly or decorous to ignore a subject which is so deeply interesting to thousands of our countrymen." In speaking of the doctrines of the socialists, the writer goes on to say: "The position they take is this: Society is altogether out of joint. Its anomalies, its disfigured aspect, its glaring inequalities, the sufferings of the most numerous portions of it, are monstrous, indefensible, and yearly increasing. Mere palliations, mere sham improvements, mere gradual ameliorations will not meet its wants; it must be remodelled, not merely furbished up. Political economy has hitherto had it all its own way; and the shocking condition into which it has brought us, shews that its principles must be strangely inadequate or unsound. The miseries of the great mass of the people, the inability to find work, or to obtain in return for such work as can be performed in reasonable time and by ordinary strength a sufficiency of the comforts and necessaries of life, may all be traced to one source—competition instead of combination. The antagonistic and regenerative principle which must be introduced, is association." No association, no efficient combination of labor can be effected till men give up their liberty of action and subject themselves to a common despotic head or ruler. This is slavery, and towards this socialism is moving. The above quotation and the succeeding one go to prove the positions with which we set out: that free trade or political economy is the science of free society, and socialism the science of slavery. The writer from whom we are quoting sees and thus exposes the tendency of socialism to slavery: "There is the usual jumble between the fourteenth century and the nineteenth; the desire to recall the time when the poor were at once the serfs and the proteges of the rich, and to amalgamate it with the days of chartism, when the poor assert their equality and insist upon their freedom. It is not thus that irritation can be allayed or miseries removed or wrongs redressed. The working classes and their advocates must decide on which of the two positions they will take their stand: whether they will be cared for as dependents and inferiors, or whether, by wisdom, self-control, frugality and toil, they will fight their independent way to dignity and well-being; whether they will step back to a stationary and degraded past, or strive onward to the assertion of their free humanity? But it is not given to them, any more than to other classes, to combine inconsistent advantages: they cannot unite the safety of being in leading strings, with the liberty of being without them; the right of acting for themselves, with the right to be saved from the consequences of their actions; they must not whine because the higher classes do not aid them, and refuse to let these classes direct them; they must not insist on the duty of government to provide for them, and deny the authority of government to control them; they must not denounce *laissez-faire*, and denounce a paternal despotism likewise." The greatest of all communists, if communist he be, Proudhon, has also seen and exposed this tendency of socialism to slavery. He is a thorough-going enemy of modern free society; calls property a thief; and would, he says, establish anarchy in place of government. But we have not been able to understand his system, if any he has.

The North British Review stands probably as high for its ability, sound political views and literary integrity, as any other periodical whatever. We will cite copiously from its article on "Literature and the Labor Question," February No. 1851, not merely for the weight of its authority and the force of its arguments, but chiefly because the writer of that article sums up with some fulness and great ability the proofs of the failure of society as now constituted in Western Europe, and of the almost universal abandonment of political economy, the philosophy of that society :

"Servants of this class, and constituting by far the most numerous portion of every community, are the *prolétaires*, or speaking more restrictedly, the working men, who earn to-day's bread by to-day's labor. They are the veritable descendants of those who in ancient times were the slaves; with but few differences their social position is the same. Despite saving banks, temperance societies, and institutions for mutual improvement, the characteristics of this class, like that of the literary class, is, and probably ever will be, pecuniary *insouciance*. From week to week, these thousands live, now in work and now out of work, as careless of to-morrow as if Benjamin Franklin had never lived, entering at one end of the jour-

ney of existence and issuing at the other, without
ever having at any one moment accumulated five
superfluous shillings."

A beautiful commentary on the dignity of labor.

As to the prevalence of discontent with free
society, and of socialistic and revolutionary doctrines in France, the writer employs the following
language:

"One cannot now take up a French book-seller's
list of advertisements, without seeing the titles of
publications of all kinds and sizes devoted to the
elucidation of social questions. 'L'Organization
du Travail;' 'Destinie Sociale;' 'Etudes sur la
principales causes de la Misere;' 'De la condition
physique and morale des jeune Ouvriens.' Such
are some of the titles of a class of French books
sufficient already to form a library. The thing, in
fact, has become a profession in France. Men of
all kinds and of all capacities—men who do not
care one farthing about the condition of the people,
or about the condition of any body except themselves, as well as men of real goodness and philanthropy, now write books full of statistics about
the working classes, and of plans for diminishing
the amount of social evil. And so too in this
country. The 'Condition of England Question'
has become the target at which every shallow wit-
ling must aim his shaft. All literature seems to be
flowing towards this channel, so that there seems

to be a likelihood that we shall soon have no literature at all but a literature of social reference."

Whilst all this hubbub and confusion is going on in France and England, occasioned by the intensest suffering of the free laborers, we of the South and of all slaveholding countries, have been "calm as a summer's evening," quite unconscious of the storm brewing around us. Yet those people who confess that their situation is desperate, insist that we shall imitate their institutions, starve our laborers, multiply crime, riots and pauperism, in order, we suppose, to try the experiment of Mormonism, Socialism or Communism. Try it first, yourselves!

The following passage—and we have quoted a similar one from Blackwood—is a distinct assertion of the complete failure of free society. It is the admission of witnesses of the highest character, corroborated by the testimony of all classes of society—for the poor, by their strikes, trade unions, temperance societies, odd-fellow societies, and insurance societies, speak as eloquently on this subject as the rich and the learned.

" 'Alton Locke' is, upon the whole, as powerful a literary expression as exists of the *general conviction*, shared by all classes alike, that the country has arrived at a condition when something extraordinary, whatever it is, must be decided on and done, if society is to be saved in Great Britain.

As such, therefore, it is a book that should be welcome to all parties."

Now listen to the conclusion, and see whether the practical remedy proposed be not SLAVERY. We believe there is not an intelligent reformist in the world who does not see the necessity of slavery—who does not advocate its re-institution in all save the name. Every one of them concurs in deprecating free competition, and in the wish and purpose to destroy it. To destroy it is to destroy Liberty, and where liberty is destroyed, slavery is established.

"At what conclusion have we arrived? We have pointed out as one of the most remarkable signs of the times, the appearance of a literature of social reference, originating in and then farther promoting a *repprochement* between the two extremes of society, men of letters and the working classes. We have examined, and to some extent analyzed, the two most conspicuous examples that have been recently furnished in this country, of this new direction and intention of literature. And what has been the result? The result has been, that in both cases, we have found ourselves conducted by the writers in question to one point: the pronunciation of the terrible phrase, 'Organization of Labor,' and the contemplation of a possible exodus, at no very - distant period, out of the Egypt of our present system, of *competition and laissez-faire,* into a comparative Canaan of some kind of co-operative socialism. Such is the fact: startling it may be, but deserving to be fairly stated and apprehended. Right or wrong, we believe this to be a true version and fair history of our current social literature. We have elicited it from an examination of but two examples; but we believe the most extensive examination would not invalidate it. Collect all the books, pamphlets and papers that constitute our literature of social reference, or assemble all our men of letters, who have contributed to that literature, so as to learn their private aspirations and opinions with respect to the social problem, and the last word, the united note would still be: ' The Organization of Labor on the associative principle.' There are of course dissentients, but such is the note of the majority; and so far as the note is of value, it may be asserted that a decree of the literary faculty of the country has gone forth, declaring the avater of political economy, if not as a science of facts, at least as a supreme rule of government, to be near its close."

Now strip these and the extracts from Blackwood of their pompous verbiage, and they become express assertions that free society has failed, and that that which is not free must be substituted. Every Southern slave has an estate in tail, indefeasible by fine and recovery, in the lands of the

South. If his present master cannot support him, he must sell him to one who can. Slaves, too, have a valuable property in their masters. Abolitionists overlook this—overlook the protective influence of slavery, its distinguishing feature, and no doubt the cause of its origin and continuance, and abuse it as a mere engine of oppression. Infant negroes, sick, helpless, aged and infirm negres, are simply a charge to their master; he has no property in them in the common sense of the term, for they are of no value for the time, but they have the most invaluable property in him. He is bound to support them, to supply all their wants, and relieve them of all care for the present or future. And well, and feelingly and faithfully does he discharge his duty. What a glorious thing to man is slavery, when want, misfortune, old age, debility and sickness overtake him. Free society, in its various forms of insurance, in its odd-fellow and temperance societies, in its social and communistic establishments, and in ten thousand other ways, is vainly attempting to attain this never-failing protective, care-taking and supporting feature of slavery. But it will blunder and flounder on in vain. It cannot put a heart and feeling into its societies and its corporations. God makes masters and gives them affections, feelings and interests that secure kindness to the sick, aged and dying slave. Man can never inspire his ricketty

institutions with those feelings, interests and affections. Say the Abolitionists—"Man ought not to
have property in man." What a dreary, cold,
bleak, inhospitable world this would be with such
a doctrine carried into practice. Men living to
themselves, like owls and wolves and lions and
birds and beasts of prey? No: "Love thy neighbor as thyself." And this can't be done till he
has a property in your services as well as a place
in your heart. *Homo sum, humani nihil a me
alienum puto!* This, the noblest sentiment ever
uttered by uninspired man, recognises the great
truth which lies at the foundation of all society—
that every man has property in his fellow-man!
It is because that adequate provision is not made
properly to enforce this great truth in free society,
that men are driven to the necessity of attempting
to remedy the defects of government by voluntary
assocations, that carry into definite and practical
operation this great and glorious truth. It is because such defects do not exist in slave society,
that we are not troubled with strikes, trade unions,
phalasteries, communistic establishments, Mormonism, and the thousand other isms that deface and
deform free society. Socialism, in some form or
other, is universal in free society, and its single
aim is to attain the protective influence of slavery.
St. Simon would govern his social establishments
by savants, more despotic than masters. He would

have no law but the will of the savant. He would have a despot without the feelings and the interests of a master to temper his authority. Fourier proposes some wild plan of passional attraction as a substitute for government, and Louis Blanc is eloquent about "attractive labor." All human experience proves that society must be ruled not by mere abstractions, but by men of flesh and blood. To attain large industrial results, it must be vigorously and severely ruled. Socialism is already slavery in all save the master. It had as well adopt that feature at once, as come to that it must to make its schemes at once humane and efficient. Socialism in other forms than that of slavery is not a new thing. It existed in Crete, in Sparta, in Peru, and was practiced by the Essenes in Judea. All ancient institutions were very much tinged with its doctrines and practices, not only in the relation of master and slave, which was universal, but in the connection of the free citizens to one another and to the government. The doctrines of individuality, of the social contract and of *laissez-faire*, had not then arisen. Our only quarrel with Socialism is, that it will not honestly admit that it owes its recent revival to the failure of universal liberty, and is seeking to bring about slavery again in some form.

The little experiment of universal liberty that has been tried for a little while in a little corner of Europe, has resulted in disastrous and appalling failure. Slavery has been too universal not to be necessary to nature, and man struggles in vain against nature. "Expel nature with a fork, and she will again return;" or, in the eloquent language of Solomon—"The thing that hath been, it is that that shall be; and that which is done, is that which shall be done; and there is no new thing under the sun."

No one who reads a newspaper can but have observed that every abolitionist is either an agrarian, a socialist, an infidel, an anti-renter, or in some way is trying to upset other institutions of society, as well as slavery at the South. The same reasoning that makes him an abolitionist soon carries him further, for he finds slavery in some form so interwoven with the whole frame-work of society, that he invariably ends by proposing to destroy the whole edifice and building another on entirely new principles. Some, like Fourier, are honest enough to admit that it must also be built with new materials. There is too much human nature in man for their purposes. Part of that nature is the continual effort to make others work and support him whilst he is idle; in other words, to enslave them, and yet not be charged with their support. But Fourier and his disciples promise most positively that their system will in a few generations cleanse mankind of their mundane dross, expel every particle of human nature, and that then their system will work admirably. Until then, we would advise them to procure good practical overseers from Virginia to govern their phalanxes and phalasteries; and we venture to affirm, if they try one, they will never be willing to exchange him for that whip-syllabub, sentimental ruler, " passional attraction." Passional attraction is the very thing government has chiefly to check and punish, and we suspect it will be so to the end of the chapter. The argument seems fairly, however, to have arrived at this point: All concur that free society is a failure. We slaveholders say you must recur to domestic slavery, the oldest, the best and most common form of Socialism. The new schools of Socialism promise something better, but admit, to obtain that something, they must first destroy and eradicate man's human nature.

CHAPTER III.

SUBJECT CONTINUED.

"There was a time,
That when the brains were out, the man would die!"

Cotemporaneously with the explosion of his favorite theory, Mr. Calhoun folded his robe around him with imperial dignity, and expired in the arms of an admiring Senate. Mr. Macaulay and the Edinburgh Review still cling to life with the querulous pertinacity of a pair of cats. "Othello's occupation's gone!" Why does Othello still linger on the stage?

Since writing our last chapter, the Edinburgh Review for July, 1854, has reached us. It contains a critique on "An Essay on the Relations between Labor and Capital. B. C. Morrison." The failure of free society we think is admitted in that article. We think the writer further admits that it cannot work successfully without a radical change in human nature. The remedy suggested is very simple; chronic and complex as the diseases are which it proposes to cure, yet that remedy requires the poor to give up the use of stimulants. We do not think with Lord Byron, "that man being reasonable should get drunk." We think, on the contrary, it is the most irrational act in

D

the world. But change the line a little, and it is true: "Man being *natural*, will get drunk." Any theory of society founded on the disuse of stimulants by the poor, is Utopian and false. At all events, it involves the necessity of a total change in man's nature, for men have ever used stimulants, and until such change will ever use them. If the grog and tobacco rations were withdrawn, would not a smaller number of laborers do the work that a larger number do now, and thus throw a number out of employment? When capitalists discovered that laborers could live on less than they do now, would they not reduce their wages? Would not famine be more common, when there was no room for retrenchment, no tobacco and liquor to substitute for bread, when bread rose in price? Such is the theory of Smith and Mc-Culloch, who attribute famines in Ireland to the too great economy of the peasant. We think the proposed remedy would aggravate the disease; but it suffices for our purpose, that the disease is admitted. The failure of *laissez-faire*, of political economy, is admitted now by its last and lingering votary. Free society stands condemned by the unanimous testimony of all its enlightened members. We will proceed to quote from the article on which we are commenting:

"A few years ago, when distress among our working people, if not general, was at least *chronic and severe,* when the public mind was at once crowded by startling disclosures of misery, and distracted by still more startling projects for relieving it, the book before us would have excited immediate and extensive attention. A few years hence, probably, when the stirring excitement and the noble enterprise of war shall have again given place to the more beneficent pursuits of peace, and when possibly a check to our prosperous career, arising out of war, shall have again awakened our vigilance to those symptoms of *social disorder* which we are apt to neglect in ordinary times, the book may take the rank it appears to us to deserve. * * * In truth, the great problem it proposes to discuss and elucidate is one of more permanent and mighty interest than any other, however much transient convulsions may throw it into the back-ground, or transient intervals of repose and comfort may lull us into the belief that it is solved or shelved. It is not long since public attention was thoroughly aroused to all that was *deplorable, indefensible* and *dangerous* in the condition of the *mass* of the population; we were daily made aware, that as a fact, the supply of labor was usually in excess of the demand, and that much local and occasional suffering was the consequence; but it was not till the Irish famine, and the similar visitation in the Western Highlands, the severe distresses in the manufacturing districts of England in 1847 and 1848, and the painful and undeniable, even though over-colored, revelations of the state of many thousand artisans of various trades in the metropolis, had alarmed us into inquiry and reflection, that the public mind began to comprehend either the magnitude and imminence of the evil it had to investigate, or the difficulty and complication of the problem it was called upon to solve."

The reviewer and the reviewed very successfully show, after this, that a *movement* of the laboring class would be attended with more danger in Great Britain than any where else, because in Great Britain this class compose nine-tenths of the nation. In France, where lands are minutely divided, the conservative interest preponderates. There are thirty thousand land-holders in England, three thousand in Scotland, and eleven millions in France. The state of society in Great Britain is pregnant with disastrous change and revolution. Emigration affords a temporary vent and relief, but emigration may cease, and then this complex and difficult social problem will recur. The laboring class are about to assume the reins of government. They know their own numbers and strength. All the reasoning in the world will not satisfy them that they who produce every thing should starve, in order that a handful of lords and capitalists should live in wanton waste and idle luxury. Mr. Morrison will not persuade them that it is a high crime and misdemeanor for them to use a little beer and tobacco, for they make every ounce of tobacco and pint of beer that is consumed in the kingdom. A social revolution is at hand. Dr. Sangrado could not arrest it with his "bleeding and warm water," much less Mr. Morrison with his cold water remedy. The teetotalers should give him a brass medal, for they, like he, propose to remedy all the evils that human flesh is heir to, with abstinence and cold water. The Homeopathists will dispute with the Hydropathists the propriety of conferring on him an honorary title. His infinitesimal dose ranking him with the former, and its ingredient, cold water, allying him with the latter practitioners. The reviewer admits that Great Britain is in danger of a far worse social revolution than ever visited France, and has no preventive to suggest except to stop the "grog ration." -Now, slavery is the only thing in the world that can enforce temperance. The army and navy are the only reliable temperance societies in Great Britain. Men who have lost self-control enlist in them to be controlled by superior authority. They often prolong their lives thereby. Slaves, like soldiers and sailors, are temperate, because temperance is enforced on them. If free laborers will use too much grog and tobacco, it proves they are not ripe for freedom.

But we will forego and give up every word of proof that we have deduced from history to shew the failure of free society. In the present and preceding chapters, we know we have adduced sufficient historical evidence of that failure, but we forego all that. We take a single admission of this reviewer—"that the supply of labor is usually in excess of the demand." The admission of course only applies to Great Britain, but it is well known that in free continental Europe the excess is still greater. Now, is it necessary for us to do more than state the admission to prove that free society is absurd and impracticable? Part of the laboring class are out of employment and actually starving, and in their struggle to get employment, reducing to the minimum of what will support human existence those next above them who are employed. This next and employed class are the needle-women, and coarse and common male laborers. The two classes and their dependents constitute one-half of mankind. Theoretically, this half of mankind is always at starvation point in free society. Practically, the proportion of the suffering destitute is much greater. We are astounded that conclusions so obviously and immediately resulting from admitted premises, should not have occurred to every one, especially when horrid facts beckoned the way to the conclusion.

This whole article in the Edinburgh is unfeeling and libellous, unjust and untrue. The greatest destitution and pauperism excludes the use of stimulants. The working women suffer most, and they use few stimulants. The starving peasantry of Scotland, France and Ireland, can rarely indulge in them. It is the well-paid laborers who, after the excessive fatigues of the day, indulge in the pipe and the bottle. Fatigued, maddened and desperate with the prospect before them, some little charity should be extended to their feelings. Such wholesale abuse of the laboring class will but precipitate the social revolution which the reviewer dreads.

CHAPTER IV.

THE TWO PHILOSOPHIES.

In the three preceding chapters we have shewn that the world is divided between two philosophies. The one the philosophy of free trade and universal liberty—the philosophy adapted to promote the interests of the strong, the wealthy and the wise. The other, that of socialism, intended to protect the weak, the poor and the ignorant. The latter is almost universal in free society; the former prevails in the slaveholding States of the South. Thus we see each section cherishing theories at war with existing institutions. The people of the North and of Europe are pro-slavery men in the abstract; those of the South are theoretical abolitionists. This state of opinions is readily accounted for. The people in free society feel the evils of universal liberty and free competition, and desire to get rid of those evils. They propose a remedy, which is in fact slavery; but they are wholly unconscious of what they are doing, because never having lived in the midst of slavery, they know not what slavery is. The citizens of the South, who have seen none of the evils of liberty and competition, but just enough of those agencies to operate as healthful stimulants to energy, enterprise and industry, believe free competition to be an unmixed good.

The South, quiet, contented, satisfied, looks upon all socialists and radical reformers as madmen or knaves. It is as ignorant of free society as that society is of slavery. Each section sees one side of the subject alone; each, therefore, takes partial and erroneous views of it. Social science will never take a step in advance till some Southern slaveholder, competent for the task, devotes a life-time to its study and elucidation; for slavery can only be understood by living in its midst, whilst thousands of books daily exhibit the minutest workings of free society. The knowledge of the numerous theories of radical reform proposed in Europe, and the causes that have led to their promulgation, is of vital importance to us. Yet we turn away from them with disgust, as from something unclean and vicious. We occupy high vantage ground for observing, studying and classifying the various phenomena of society; yet we do not profit by the advantages of our position. We should do so, and indignantly hurl back upon our assailants the charge, that there is something wrong and rotten in our system. From their own mouths we can show free society to be a monstrous abortion, and slavery to be the healthy, beautiful and natural being which they are trying, unconsciously, to adopt.

CHAPTER V.

NEGRO SLAVERY.

We have already stated that we should not attempt to introduce any new theories of government and of society, but merely try to justify old ones, so far as we could deduce such theories from ancient and almost universal practices. Now it has been the practice in all countries and in all ages, in some degree, to accommodate the amount and character of government control to the wants, intelligence, and moral capacities of the nations or individuals to be governed. A highly moral and intellectual people, like the free citizens of ancient Athens, are best governed by a democracy. For a less moral and intellectual one, a limited and constitutional monarchy will answer. For a people either very ignorant or very wicked, nothing short of military despotism will suffice. So among individuals, the most moral and well-informed members of society require no other government than law. They are capable of reading and understanding the law, and have sufficient self-control and virtuous disposition to obey it. Children cannot be governed by mere law; first, because they do not understand it, and secondly, because they are so much under the influence of impulse, passion and appetite, that they want sufficient self-control to be deterred or governed by the distant and doubtful penalties of the law. They must be constantly controlled by parents or guardians, whose will and orders shall stand in the place of law for them. Very wicked men must be put into penitentiaries; lunatics into asylums, and the most wild of them into straight jackets, just as the most wicked of the sane are manacled with irons; and idiots must have committees to govern and take care of them. Now, it is clear the Athenian democracy would not suit a negro nation, nor will the government of mere law suffice for the individual negro. He is but a grown up child, and must be governed as a child, not as a lunatic or criminal. The master occupies towards him the place of parent or guardian. We shall not dwell on this view, for no one will differ with us who thinks as we do of the negro's capacity, and we might argue till dooms-day, in vain, with those who have a high opinion of the negro's moral and intellectual capacity.

Secondly. The negro is improvident; will not lay up in summer for the wants of winter; will not accumulate in youth for the exigencies of age. He would become an insufferable burden to society. Society has the right to prevent this, and can only do so by subjecting him to domestic slavery.

In the last place, the negro race is inferior to the white race, and living in their midst, they would be far outstripped or outwitted in the chase of free competition. Gradual but certain extermination would be their fate. We presume the maddest abolitionist does not think the negro's providence of habits and money-making capacity at all to compare to those of the whites. This defect of character would alone justify enslaving him, if he is to remain here. In Africa or the West Indies, he would become idolatrous, savage and cannibal, or be devoured by savages and cannibals. At the North he would freeze or starve.

We would remind those who deprecate and sympathize with negro slavery, that his slavery here relieves him from a far more cruel slavery in Africa, or from idolatry and cannibalism, and every brutal vice and crime that can disgrace humanity; and that it christianizes, protects, supports and civilizes him; that it governs him far better than free laborers at the North are governed. There, wife-murder has become a mere holiday pastime; and where so many wives are murdered, almost all must be brutally treated. Nay, more: men who kill their wives or treat them brutally, must be ready for all kinds of crime, and the calendar of crime at the North proves the inference to be correct. Negroes never kill their wives. If it be objected that legally they have no wives, then we reply, that in an experience of more than forty years, we never yet heard of a negro man killing a negro woman. Our negroes are not only better off as to physical comfort than free laborers, but their moral condition is better.

But abolish negro slavery, and how much of slavery still remains. Soldiers and sailors in Europe enlist for life; here, for five years. Are they not slaves who have not only sold their liberties, but their lives also? And they are worse treated than domestic slaves. No domestic affection and self-interest extend their ægis over them. No kind mistress, like a guardian angel, provides for them in health, tends them in sickness, and soothes their dying pillow. Wellington at Waterloo was a slave. He was bound to obey, or would, like admiral Byng, have been shot for gross misconduct, and might not, like a common laborer, quit his work at any moment. He had sold his liberty, and might not resign without the consent of his master, the king. The common laborer may quit his work at any moment, whatever his contract; declare that liberty is an inalienable right, and leave his employer to redress by a useless suit for damages. The highest and most honorable position on earth was that of the slave Wellington; the lowest, that of the free man who cleaned his boots and fed his hounds. The Afri-

can cannibal, caught, christianized and enslaved,
is as much elevated by slavery as was Wellington. The kind of slavery is adapted to the men
enslaved. Wives and apprentices are slaves; not
in theory only, but often in fact. Children are
slaves to their parents, guardians and teachers.
Imprisoned culprits are slaves. Lunatics and
idiots are slaves also. Three-fourths of free society are slaves, no better treated, when their
wants and capacities are estimated, than negro
slaves. The masters in free society, or slave society, if they perform properly their duties, have
more cares and less liberty than the slaves themselves. "In the sweat of thy face shalt thou earn
thy bread!" made all men slaves, and such all
good men continue to be.

Negro slavery would be changed immediately
to some form of peonage, serfdom or villienage, if the negroes were sufficiently intelligent
and provident to manage a farm. No one would
have the labor and trouble of management, if
his negroes would pay in hires and rents one-
half what free tenants pay in rent in Europe.
Every negro in the South would be soon liberated,
if he would take liberty on the terms that white
tenants hold it. The fact that he cannot enjoy
liberty on such terms, seems conclusive that he is
only fit to be a slave.

But for the assaults of the abolitionists, much
would have been done ere this to regulate and

improve Southern slavery. Our negro mechanics
do not work so hard, have many more privileges
and holidays, and are better fed and clothed than
field hands, and are yet more valuable to their
masters. The slaves of the South are cheated of
their rights by the purchase of Northern manufactures which they could produce. Besides, if we
would employ our slaves in the coarser processes
of the mechanic arts and manufactures, such as
brick making, getting and hewing timber for ships
and houses, iron mining and smelting, coal mining,
grading railroads and plank roads, in the manufacture of cotton, tobacco, &c., we would find
a vent in new employments for their increase,
more humane and more profitable than the vent
afforded by new states and territories. The nice
and finishing processes of manufactures and mechanics should be reserved for the whites, who
only are fitted for them, and thus, by diversifying
pursuits and cutting off dependence on the North,
we might benefit and advance the interests of our
whole population. Exclusive agriculture has de-
pressed and impoverished the South. We will not
here dilate on this topic, because we intend to
make it the subject of a separate essay. Free
trade doctrines, not slavery, have made the South
agricultural and dependent, given her a sparse and
ignorant population, ruined her cities, and expelled
her people.

Would the abolitionists approve of a system of society that set white children free, and remitted them at the age of fourteen, males and females, to all the rights, both as to person and property, which belong to adults? Would it be criminal or praiseworthy to do so? Criminal, of course. Now, are the average of negroes equal in information, in native intelligence, in prudence or providence, to well-informed white children of fourteen? We who have lived with them for forty years, think not. The competition of the world would be too much for the children. They would be cheated out of their property and debased in their morals. Yet they would meet every where with sympathizing friends of their own color, ready to aid, advise and assist them. The negro would be exposed to the same competition and greater temptations, with no greater ability to contend with them, with these additional difficulties. He would be welcome nowhere; meet with thousands of enemies and no friends. If he went North, the white laborers would kick him and cuff him, and drive him out o employment. If he went to Africa, the savages would cook him and eat him. If he went to the West Indies, they would not let him in, or if they did, they would soon make of him a savage and idolater.

We have a further question to ask. If it be right and incumbent to subject children to the authority of parents and guardians, and idiots and lunatics to committees, would it not be equally right and incumbent to give the free negroes masters, until at least they arrive at years of discretion, which very few ever did or will attain? What is the difference between the authority of a parent and of a master? Neither pay wages, and each is entitled to the services of those subject to him. The father may not sell his child forever, but may hire him out till he is twenty-one. The free negro's master may also be restrained from selling. Let him stand in *loco parentis*, and call him papa instead of master. Look closely into slavery, and you will see nothing so hideous in it; or if you do, you will find plenty of it at home in its most hideous form.

The earliest civilization of which history gives account is that of Egypt. The negro was always in contact with that civilization. For four thousand years he has had opportunities of becoming civilized. Like the wild horse, he must be caught, tamed and domesticated. When his subjugation ceases he again runs wild, like the cattle on the Pampas of the South, or the horses on the prairies of the West. His condition in the West Indies proves this.

It is a common remark, that the grand and lasting architectural structures of antiquity were the results of slavery. The mighty and continued association of labor requisite to their construction, when mechanic art was so little advanced, and labor-saving processes unknown, could only have been brought about by a despotic authority, like that of the master over his slaves. It is, however, very remarkable, that whilst in taste and artistic skill the world seems to have been retrograding ever since the decay and abolition of feudalism, in mechanical invention and in great utilitarian operations requiring the wielding of immense capital and much labor, its progress has been unexampled. Is it because capital is more despotic in its authority over free laborers than Roman masters and feudal lords were over their slaves and vassals?

Free society has continued long enough to justify the attempt to generalize its phenomena, and calculate its moral and intellectual influences. It is obvious that, in whatever is purely utilitarian and material, it incites invention and stimulates industry. Benjamin Franklin, as a man and a philosopher, is the best exponent of the working of the system. His sentiments and his philosophy are low, selfish, atheistic and material. They tend directly to make man a mere " featherless biped," well-fed, well-clothed and comfortable, but regardless of his soul as "the beasts that perish."

Since the Reformation the world has as regularly been retrograding in whatever belongs to the departments of genius, taste and art, as it has been progressing in physical science and its application to mechanical construction. Mediæval Italy rivalled if it did not surpass ancient Rome, in poetry, in sculpture, in painting, and many of the fine arts. Gothic architecture reared its monuments of skill and genius throughout Europe, till the 15th century; but Gothic architecture died with the Reformation. The age of Elizabeth was the Augustan age of England. The men who lived then acquired their sentiments in a world not yet deadened and vulgarized by puritanical cant and levelling demagoguism. Since then men have arisen who have been the fashion and the go for a season, but none have appeared whose names will descend to posterity. Liberty and equality made slower advances in France. The age of Louis XIV. was the culminating point of French genius and art. It then shed but a flickering and lurid light. Frenchmen are servile copyists of Roman art, and Rome had no art of her own. She borrowed from Greece; distorted and deteriorated what she borrowed; and France imitates and falls below Roman distortions. The genius of Spain disappeared with Cervantes; and now the world seems to regard nothing as desirable except what will make money and what costs money. There is not a poet, an orator, a sculptor, or painter in the world. The tedious elaboration necessary to all the productions of high art would be ridiculed

in this money-making, utilitarian, charlatan age.
Nothing now but what is gaudy and costly excites
admiration. The public taste is debased.

But far the worst feature of modern civilization,
which is the civilization of free society, remains to
be exposed. Whilst labor-saving processes have
probably lessened by one half, in the last century,
the amount of work needed for comfortable support, the free laborer is compelled by capital and
competition to work more than he ever did before,
and is less comfortable. The organization of society cheats him of his earnings, and those earnings go to swell the vulgar pomp and pageantry
of the ignorant millionaires, who are the only
great of the present day. These reflections might
seem, at first view, to have little connexion with
negro slavery; but it is well for us of the South
not to be deceived by the tinsel glare and glitter
of free society, and to employ ourselves in doing
our duty at home, and studying the past, rather
than in insidious rivalry of the expensive pleasures
and pursuits of men whose sentiments and whose
aims are low, sensual and grovelling.

Human progress, consisting in moral and intellectual improvement, and there being no agreed
and conventional standard weights or measures of
moral and intellectual qualities and quantities, the
question of progress can never be accurately decided. We maintain that man has not improved,

because in all save the mechanic arts he reverts to the distant past for models to imitate, and he never imitates what he can excel.

We need never have white slaves in the South, because we have black ones. Our citizens, like those of Rome and Athens, are a privileged class. We should train and educate them to deserve the privileges and to perform the duties which society confers on them. Instead, by a low demagoguism depressing their self-respect by discourses on the equality of man, we had better excite their pride by reminding them that they do not fulfil the menial offices which white men do in other countries. Society does not feel the burden of providing for the few helpless paupers in the South. And we should recollect that here we have but half the people to educate, for half are negroes; whilst at the North they profess to educate all. It is in our power to spike this last gun of the abolitionists. We should educate all the poor. The abolitionists say that it is one of the necessary consequences of slavery that the poor are neglected. It was not so in Athens, and in Rome, and should not be so in the South. If we had less trade with and less dependence on the North, all our poor might be profitably and honorably employed in trades, professions and manufactures. Then we should have a rich and denser population. Yet we but marshal her in the way that she was going. The South is

already aware of the necessity of a new policy,
and has begun to act on it. Every day more and
more is done for education, the mechanic arts,
manufactures and internal improvements. We will
soon be independent of the North.

We deem this peculiar question of negro slavery
of very little importance. The issue is made
throughout the world on the general subject of
slavery in the abstract. The argument has commenced. One set of ideas will govern and control
after awhile the civilized world. Slavery will every
where be abolished, or every where be re-instituted.
We think the opponents of practical, existing
slavery, are estopped by their own admission;
nay, that unconsciously, as socialists, they are the
defenders and propagandists of slavery, and have
furnished the only sound arguments on which its
defence and justification can be rested. We have
introduced the subject of negro slavery to afford
us a better opportunity to disclaim the purpose of
reducing the white man any where to the condition
of negro slaves here. It would be very unwise
and unscientific to govern white men as you would
negroes. Every shade and variety of slavery has
existed in the world. In some cases there has
been much of legal regulation, much restraint of
the master's authority; in others, none at all.
The character of slavery necessary to protect the
whites in Europe should be much milder than

negro slavery, for slavery is only needed to protect the white man, whilst it is more necessary for
the government of the negro even than for his
protection. But even negro slavery should not be
outlawed. We might and should have laws in
Virginia, as in Louisiana, to make the master subject to presentment by the grand jury and to punishment, for any inhuman or improper treatment
or neglect of his slave.

We abhor the doctrine of the "Types of Mankind;" first, because it is at war with scripture,
which teaches us that the whole human race is
descended from a common parentage; and, secondly, because it encourages and incites brutal
masters to treat negroes, not as weak, ignorant
and dependent brethren, but as wicked beasts,
without the pale of humanity. The Southerner is
the negro's friend, his only friend. Let no inter-
meddling abolitionist, no refined philosophy, dis-
solve this friendship.

CHAPTER VI.

SCRIPTURAL AUTHORITY FOR SLAVERY.

We find slavery repeatedly instituted by God, or by men acting under his immediate care and direction, as in the instances of Moses and Joshua. Nowhere in the Old or New Testament do we find the institution condemned, but frequently recognized and enforced. In individual instances slavery may be treated as an evil, and no doubt it is often a very great one where its subject is fitted to take care of himself and would be happier and more useful as a freeman than as a slave. It was often imposed as a punishment for sin, but this affords no argument against its usefulness or its necessity. It is probably no cause of regret that men are so constituted as to require that many should be slaves. Slavery opens many sources of happiness and occasions and encourages the exercise of many virtues and affections which would be unknown without it. It begets friendly, kind and affectionate relations, just as equality engenders antagonism and hostility on all sides. The condition of slavery in all ages and in all countries has been considered in the general disgraceful, but so to some extent have hundreds of the necessary trades and occupations of freemen. The necessity which often compels the best of men to resort to such trades and occupations in no degree degrades their character, nor does the necessity which imposes slavery degrade the character of the slave. The man who acts well his part, whether as slave or free laborer, is entitled to and commands the esteem and respect of all good men. The disgrace of slavery all consists in the cowardice, the improvidence or crime which generally originate it. The Babylonian captivity and slavery were intended to chastise, purify and elevate the Jews, not to degrade them. The disgrace consisted in the crimes, the effeminacy and the idolatry which invited and occasioned that captivity.

If the scriptural authority for slavery were robbed of its divine authorship, still it would stand far above all human authority. Moses, if an impostor, was the wisest statesman that ever lived. Under his stereotyped and unchangeable institutions, Judea, a small and barren country, went on to prosper, until in the age of Solomon, the Jews became the wealthiest and most enlightened people on earth. More than a thousand years afterwards, in the reign of Vespasian, the single city of Jerusalem defied for six months the combined power of the civilized world, led on by the best warrior and greatest genius of the age.

Such vitality did those institutions of Moses

E

possess, that although the Jews were scattered in after times to the four winds of heaven, down trodden, hated, persecuted, oppressed, still clinging to the very letter of his law, they are to day a great, numerous and prosperous people. Whilst the lower classes among them are shrewd, cunning, filthy and dishonest, the upper classes are honest, highminded, enlightened and immensely wealthy. Today, the Rothschilds wield as much power as the Emperor Nicholas, and wield it more wisely and humanely. Of their institutions slavery was an important element. If their unparalleled wisdom and success prove not their divine origin, this at least proves that they are infinitely the best models of human polity.

Ham, a son of Noah, was condemned to slavery and his posterity after him. We do not adopt the theory that he was the ancestor of the negro race. The Jewish slaves were not negroes, and to confine the justification of slavery to that race would be to weaken its scriptural authority, and to lose the whole weight of profane authority, for we read of no negro slavery in ancient times.

The righteous Abraham, the chosen of God from a wicked world, was both prince and master. He possessed the power of life and death over his subjects or slaves, and over his wife and children. When about to sacrifice Isaac, he never dreamed that any human authority could dispute his right or stay his hand. Yet who would not prefer to have been of the household of Abraham, to delving as a free laborer for some vulgar boss of modern times. In the times of Abraham, we may infer from his history that all masters possessed the power of life and death. It teaches us another lesson,—how much there is in a name. We attach nothing humiliating or disgraceful to the situation of the subject of a despotic prince; but call him master, " there all the *dishonor* lies." In truth, the influences on character are the same, provided the persons subjected be the same.

The first runaway we read of was Hagar, and she we find, like runaways at the North, about to perish for want. An angel of the Lord did not spurn the office which Senator Sumner contemns—to restore the fugitive to her owners. "And the Angel of the Lord said unto her, return to thy mistress and submit thyself under her hands." St. Paul, the Chevalier Bayard of Christianity, had not so nice a sense of honor as the Massachusetts Senator. He returned Onesimus to his master. Christianity then inculcated and enjoined obedience to masters. Pretended Christianity, now, incites disobedience and insurrection, and heads mobs to rescue slaves from their masters.

In Judea men might become slaves, as captives taken in war; probably a majority of slaves were of this character. It has been, on insufficient grounds we think, assumed, that slavery owes its origin generally to this source.

It is true that ancient peoples made slaves of the vanquished, but it is also true, that in all instances we find slavery pre-existing in both the conquering and conquered nation. The word "servus" is said to derive its origin from the fact that prisoners of war who were made slaves, were saved or preserved from death thereby; their lives being, according to the Law of Nations as then understood, forfeited to the victor. The Chinese every day sell themselves to each other to "save or preserve" themselves from want, hunger and death. Such instances no doubt were of daily occurrence in all ancient societies, and the word "servus" may have as well originated from this social practice as from the practices of war. We do not think history will sustain the theory that even in case of war, it was the mere saving the life, that originated the term. Conquerors in feudal times, we know, and probably in all times, parcelled out the conquered territory, both the lands and the people, to inferior chieftains, whose interest and duty it became to preserve lands, fruits, crops, houses, and inhabitants, from the cruel rapine, waste, pillage and oppression of the common soldiers. It is the interest of victors not to destroy what they have vanquished, and history shows that their usages have conformed to their interests. We deem this definition of the origin of slavery by war more consistent with history and humanity, than the usual one, that the mere life of the prisoner was saved, and hence he was called "servus."

Men might sell themselves in Judea, and they could be sold for debt or crime. The slavery of the Jews was but temporary, that of the heathen to the Jews hereditary. We cannot conclude the scriptural view of slavery better than by the citation of authorities collected and collated from the Old and New Testaments by Professor Stuart of Andover, in a pamphlet entitled, "Conscience and the Constitution."

Exodus xxi: 2. If thou buy a Hebrew servant, six years he shall serve, and he the seventh shall go out free for nothing. (3.) If he came in by himself, he shall go out by himself; if he were married, then his wife shall go out with him. (4.) If his master have given him a wife, and she have borne him sons or daughters, the wife and her children shall be her master's, and he shall go out by himself. (7.) And if a man sell his daughter to be a maid servant, she shall not go out as the men servants do. (8.) If she please not her master, who hath betrothed her to himself, then shall he let her be redeemed: to sell her unto a strange nation, he shall have no power, seeing he hath dealt deceitfully with her. (9.) And if he have betrothed her unto his son, he shall deal with her after the manner of daughters. (10.) If he take him another wife, her food, her raiment, and her duty of marriage, shall he not diminish. (11.) And if he do not these three unto her, then shall she go out free without money. (20.) And if a man smite his servant or his maid, with a rod, and he die under his hand, he shall be surely punished. (21.) Notwithstanding, if he continue a day or two, he shall not be punished: for he is his money. (26.) And if a man smite the eye of his servant or maid, that it perish, he shall let him go free for his eye's sake. (27.) And if he smite out his man servant's tooth or his maid servant's tooth; he shall let him go free for the tooth's sake.

Leviticus xxv: 44. Both thy bondmen and thy bondmaids which thou shalt have, shall be of the heathen that are around about you; of them shall you buy bondmen and bondmaids. (45.) Moreover, of the children of the strangers that do sojourn among you, of them shall ye buy, and of their families that are with you, which they begat in your land; and they shall be your possession. (46.) And ye shall take them as an *inheritance* for your children after you, to inherit them for a possession; they shall be *your bond-men forever.*

New Testament Authorities.—Paul to the Ephesians vi: 5—9. Servants, be obedient to them that are your masters according to the flesh, with fear and trembling, with singleness of heart, as unto Christ; (6.) Not with eye service as men-pleasers; but as the servants of Christ doing the will of God from the heart. (7.) With good will doing service as to the Lord, and not to men; (8.) Knowing that whatsoever good thing any man doeth, the same shall he receive of the Lord, whether he be bond or free. (9.) And ye masters, do the same thing unto them, forbearing threatening, knowing that your Master also is in heaven; neither is there respect of persons with him.

Paul, Colossians iii: 22. Servants obey in all things your masters according to the flesh; not with eye service as men-pleasers; but in singleness of heart fearing God. (23.) And whatsoever ye do, do it heartily, as to the Lord and not unto man; knowing that of the Lord ye shall receive the reward of the inheritance: for ye serve the Lord Christ. (25.) But he that doeth wrong, shall receive for the wrong which he hath done: and there is no respect of persons. (iv: 1.) Masters give unto your servants that which is just and equal, knowing that you also have a Master in heaven.

Titus ii: 9. Exhort servants to be obedient unto their own masters, and to please them well in all things; not answering again; (10.) Not purloining, but showing all good fidelity; that they may adorn the doctrine of God our Saviour in all things.

1 Peter ii: 18. Servants be subject to your masters with all fear; not only to the good and gentle, but also to the froward. (19.) For this is thank-worthy, if a man for conscience toward God endure grief, suffering wrongfully. For what glory is it, if when ye be buffetted for your faults, ye shall take it patiently? but if when ye do well and suffer for it, ye take it patiently, this is acceptable with God. (21.) For even hereunto were ye called: because Christ also suffered for us, leaving us an example that ye should follow his steps.

CHAPTER VII.

DOMESTIC AFFECTION.

Historians and philosophers, speculating upon the origin of governments, have generally agreed that the family was its first development. It has ever been, and will ever be, its most common form. Two-thirds of mankind, the women and children, are everywhere the subjects of family government. In all countries where slavery exists, the slaves also are the subjects of this kind of government. Now slaves, wives and children have no other government; they do not come directly in contact with the institutions and rulers of the State. But the family government, from its nature, has ever been despotic. The relations between the parent or master and his family subjects are too various, minute and delicate, to be arranged, defined, and enforced by law. God has in his mercy and wisdom provided a better check, to temper and direct the power of the master of the family, than any human government has devised. He who takes note of every sparrow that falls, who will not break the bruised reed, and who tempers the wind to the shorn lamb, has not been forgetful or regardless of wives, children, and slaves. He has extended the broad panoply

of domestic affection over them all, that the winds
of heaven may not visit them too roughly; under
its expansive folds other of his creatures repose
in quiet and security: the ox, the horse, the sheep,
the faithful dog, betake themselves to its friendly
shelter, and cluster around their protecting master.

Domestic affection cannot be calculated in dollars and cents. It cannot be weighed, or meas-
ured, or seen, or felt—except in its effects. "The
wind bloweth where it listeth and no man knoweth
whence it cometh or whither it goeth." Its holy
fountain is concealed in deeper recesses than the
head of the Nile, and in its course it dispenses
blessings from the rich overflowings of the heart,
ten thousand times more precious than that sacred
river ever gave to the land of Egypt. Political
economists, politicians and materialists ignore its
existence, because it is too refined for their comprehension. The material world engrosses their
attention, and they heed little those moral
agencies that Providence has established to control the material world. Slavery without domestic affection would be a curse, and so would marriage and parental authority. The free laborer
is excluded from its holy and charmed circle.
Shelterless, naked, and hungry, he is exposed to
the bleak winds, the cold rains, and hot sun of
heaven, with none that love him, none that care

for him. His employer hates him because he asks high wages or joins strikes; his fellow laborer hates him because he competes with him for employment. Foolish Abolitionists! bring him back like the Prodigal Son. Let him fare at least as well as the dog, and the horse, and the sheep. Abraham's tent is ready to receive him. Better lie down with the kids and the goats, than stand naked and hungry without. As a slave, he will be beloved and protected. Whilst free, he will be hated, despised and persecuted. Such is the will of God and order of Providence. It is idle to enquire the reasons.

Soldiers and sailors are, and ever must be, also, the subjects of despotic rule. They have sold their liberty. They have sold their persons and their lives. No domestic affection mitigates and qualifies their slavery! Those who rule them, love them not, for they belong not to their family and household. It is well that they are men in the prime of life, who can bear hard and harsh treatment; for hard and harsh treatment they are sure to get. Whipping is prohibited in the army and navy! Miserable ignorance and charlatanism! You cannot prohibit whipping until you disband both army and navy. What is whipping? Is it not corporeal punishment? and is not corporeal detention and corporeal punishment part of the sailor's and soldier's contract. If he wishes to desert, may you not and will you not restrain him by bodily force? Will you not, if necessary, knock him down, hand-cuff, and imprison him? Nay, if he repeat the offence, will you not shoot him? Will you not fasten a chain and a block to him if necessary? Whipping has not been abolished, and cannot be abolished in navy or army. Whipping means—corporeal punishment, and corporeal detention. You retain the right to inflict them, and it is a mere matter of caprice and taste how they shall be inflicted. * The man whose person is sold is a slave. The man whose person is imprisoned for punishment has felt the disgrace of whipping and endured more than its pains.

CHAPTER VIII.

RELIGION.

Our ancestors of the Revolution adopted the doctrine of free competition, demand and supply, and *Laissez-faire* in religion, as in almost everything else. The "world was too much governed," and religion seemed to them, one of the most odious forms of government. The fires of Smithfield, the Gun-powder plot, and the Vespers of St. Bartholomew were fresh in men's memories.

The Churches and lands of the Episcopal Church were confiscated. And an even-handed justice resolved that there should be no more churches, church lands, nor even burying places for the poor. Land could not be held for such purposes. They professed to allow every one to choose his own religion, but refused them a place wherein to make the selection, and to worship God after the selection should be made. No government had ever existed without a recognised state religion. To dispense with an institution so universal and so natural, was a bold experiment. Fortunately for us, Christianity did slip into our governments despite the intention of their framers. It was so interwoven with all our customs, feelings, prejudices and lives, that to the surprise and mortification of many, Christianity, though maimed, crippled and disabled, still Christianity was discovered amongst our own institutions; and probably has continued to this day the most potent and influential part of our systems.

Despite the Constitution of the United States, which secures to all the free exercise of religious freedom, there is scarcely a State in this Union that would permit, under the pretext of religious forms and observances, any gross violations of christian morality.

Mormons and Oneida Perfectionists would no sooner be tolerated in Virginia than Pyrrhic Dances and human sacrifices to Moloch. Even Catholics would not be permitted to enact a Parisian sabbath, or Venitian carnival. Christianity is the established religion of most of our States, and Christianity conforming itself to the moral feelings and prejudices of the great majority of the people. No gross violation of public decency will be allowed for the sake of false abstractions.

Women may wear paddies or bloomers, but if they carry the spirit of independence so far as to adopt a dress to conceal their sex, they will soon find themselves in a cage or a prison.

We wished to try the experiment of government without religion, we failed in the attempt. The French did try it, and enthroned the goddess of Reason hard by the reeking guillotine. Moloch might have envie'l the Goddess the number of her

victims, for the streets of Paris ran with blood.
The insane ravings of the drunken votaries of Bacchus, were innocency and decency personified, when
compared with the mad profanity of Frenchmen,
cut loose from religion, and from God.

Soon, very soon, even French republicans discovered the necessity of religion to the very existence of society and of government, and with a profanity more horrible than that which installed the
goddess of Reason, they resolved to legislate into
existence a Supreme Being. On this occasion, the
cruel Robespierre pays one of the most beautiful
and just tributes to religion we have ever read.
We quote it as a continuation of our argument
and an elucidation of our theory—" That religion
is a necessary governmental institution."

"Let us here take a lesson from history. Take
notice, I beseech you, how the men who have exercised an influence on the destinies of States
have been led into one or the other of the two opposite systems, by their personal character, and by
the very nature of their political views. Observe
with what profound art Cæsar pleading in the
Roman Senate, in behalf of the accomplices of
Cataline, deviates into a digression against the
dogma of the immortality of the human soul, so
well calculated do those ideas appear to him, to
extinguish in the hearts of the judges the energy
of virtue, so intimately does the cause of crime

seem to be connected with that of infidelity.— Cicero, on the contrary, invoked the sword of the law and the thunderbolts of the gods against the traitors. Leonidas, at Thermopylæ, supping with his companions in arms, the moment before executing the most heroic design that human virtue ever conceived, invited them for the next day to another banquet in a new life. Cato did not hesitate between Epicurus and Zeno. Brutus and the illustrious conspirators who shared his danger and his glory, belonged also to that sublime sect of the Stoics, which had such lofty ideas of the dignity of man, which carried the enthusiasm of virtue to such a height, and which was extravagant in heroism only. Stoicism saved the honor of human nature, degraded by the vices of the successors of Cæsar, and still more by the patience of the people."

In the same speech, speaking of the philosophers, he identifies atheism and materialism with the then and now prevalent doctrines of Political Economy.—" This sect propagated with great zeal the opinion of materialism, which prevailed among the great and among the *Beaux Esprits ;* to it we owe in part that kind of practical philosophy, which, reducing selfishness to a system, considers human society as a warfare of trickery, success as the rule of right and wrong, integrity as a matter of taste or decorum, the world as the atrimon of clever scoundrels."

We are gradually dismissing our political prejudice against religion. The Legislature of Virginia, some years ago, passed a law to permit religious congregations to hold land to erect churches on, and at its last session a law was enacted chartering some religious institution. The observance of the Christian sabbath is enforced by law. Ministers of the gospel are recognised as such, incapacitated to hold civil offices and exempted from many civil duties. Oaths are administered on the Bible, and infidels, it is the better opinion, are incompetent witnesses. Marriage in the South is generally a Christian ordinance as well as a civil contract, to be celebrated only by ministers of the Gospel. At the North marriage is a mere bargain, like the purchase of a horse, with the difference, that the wife cannot be swapped off—hence, when they get tired of her, they knock her on the head.

We are not surprised that frequent wife-murder should result from their low, sordid, worldly view of the marriage tie, and still less surprised, that with these, and a hundred other ill consequences arising from their sort of marriages, that women's conventions should be held to assert her rights to liberty, independence and breeches, and that sympathising bachelors in the ranks of the Socialists, propose to dispense with this troublesome and inconvenient relation altogether. In the North there is a tendency to anarchy and infidelity, in the South to conservatism and stricter religious observation. We should be cautious, prudent and experimental in giving governmental aid to religion. Like fire, if it escapes from our control, it will become dangerous and destructive,—but it is nevertheless like fire, indispensable. A republic cannot continue without the prevalence of sound morality. Laws are useless and inefficient without moral men to expound and administer them.

We have not a solitary example in all history to countenance the theories of our ancestors, that a people may be moral, or that a government can exist where religion is not in some form or degree recognised by law. What latitude shall be allowed to men in the exercise and practice of reli gion, is a question for the people to determine when the occasion requires it. It is best not to lay down abstract principles to guide us in advance. Of all the applications of philosophy none have failed so signally as when it has been tried in matters of government. Philosophy will blow up any government that is founded on it. Religion, on the other hand, will sustain the governments that rest upon it. The French build governments on *a priori* doctrines of philosophy which explode as fast as built. The English gradually and experimentally form institutions, watch their operation, and deduce general laws from those operations.

That kind of philosophy, which neither attempts to create nor account for, is admissible and useful. An extensive knowledge of the history of the various moral philosophies that have succeeded each other in the world, is useful, but only useful because it warns us to avoid all philosophy in the practical affairs of life. If we would have our people moral, and our institutions permanent, we should gradually repudiate our political abstractions and adopt religious truths in their stead.

It is an unpoplar theme to deny human progress and human improvement. We flatter ourselves that we are more enlightened as well as more moral than the ancients, yet we imitate them in all else save the mechanic arts. Our hearts, we think, are not as hard and callous as theirs, for they delighted in gladiatorial combats which would fill us with horror. But we are as much pleased to hear of victories won by our countrymen as they, and our pleasure mounts the higher as we hear of more of the enemy killed in battle. Our nerves are too delicate to witness the pangs of the dying, but we rejoice to hear they are dead. Now, our moral code is one of the purest selfishness. The ancients were divided between Stoicism and Epicurism,—the philosophy of the Sadducees and that of the Pharisees. Neither the Epicurean, nor the Sadducee professed as low, selfish and grovelling a morality as

that which our prevalent political economy inculcates. The Stoics and the Pharisees soared far above
it. Divest us of our Christian morality, and leave
us to our moral philosophy, and we might dread
the comparison with any era of the past. We
have but one moral code, and that the selfish one;
the ancients always had two, one of which was
elevated, self-denying and unselfish. In truth, a
material and infidel philosophy has prevailed for
a century, and seemed to threaten the overthrow
of Christianity. But man is a religious animal.
His mind may become distempered and diseased
for a time, and he may cavil and doubt as to
Deity, immortality and accountability—but "conscience that makes cowards of us all," soon forces
upon him the conviction that he is living in the
presence of a God. The belief in God and moral
accountability, like the belief in self-existence and
free agency, is necessitous and involuntary. It
is part of our consciousness. We cannot prove
that we exist; we cannot prove that we are free
agents. We must take our consciousness and
involuntary belief, as proof that we do exist and
are free agents. This is the conclusion at which
metaphysicians have arrived. Now explore all the
secrets of human hearts, all the recesses of history, and it will be found that religion is as much
a matter of consciousness and involuntary belief
as free agency or self-existence. It is a stubborn

fact in human nature. Statesmen cannot ignore its existence, and must provide for its exercise and enjoyment, else their institutions will vanish like chaff before the wind.

CHAPTER IX.

THE BALANCE OF TRADE.

Political economists maintain that a nation gains nothing by selling more than it buys. That the balance of trade is a humbug; nay more, that the way for a nation to get rich is to buy more than it sells. Thus more will come in than goes out. Instinct and common sénse deny the proposition. They say, that the way for individuals or people to get rich is to sell more than they buy. Philosophy beats them all hollow in argument, yet instinct and common sense are right and philosophy wrong. Philosophy is always wrong and instinct and common sense always right, because philosophy is unobservant and reasons from narrow and insufficient premises, whilst common sense sees and observes all things, giving them their due weight, comes to just conclusions, but being busied about practical every day matters, has never learned the process of abstraction, has never learned how to look into the operations of its mind and see how it has come to its conclusions. It always judges rightly, but reasons wrong. It comes to its conclusions by the same processes of ratiocination that abstract philosophers do, but unaccustomed and untrained to look into its own mental operations, it knows not how it arrived at those conclusions. It sees all the facts and concludes rightly,—abstract philosophers see but a few, reason correctly on them, but err in judgment because their premises are partial and incorrect. Men of sound judgments, are always men who give wrong reasons for their opinions. They form correct opinions because they are practical and experienced; they give wrong reasons for those opinions, because they are no abstractionists and cannot detect, follow and explain the operations of their own minds. The judgment of women is far superior to that of men. They are more calm and observant. Every married man knows that when he places a scheme before his wife and she disapproves it, he conquers her in argument, goes away distrusting his own opinion, though triumphant, and finds in the end his wife was right, though she could not tell why. Women have more sense than men, but they want courage to carry out and execute what their judgments commend. Hence men, although they fail in a thousand visionary schemes, succeed at last in some one, and are dubbed the nobler sex. An old bachelor friend of ours, says: women are great at a quarrel, bad at argument.

This is deviating a little from the balance of trade, but we return to it. All political economists contend that the local increase of currency increases prices, and Say goes so far as to say that doubling the money in France, would double prices in France. Rich men do not give double as high prices as poor men, but buy cheaper, although they have more money. Money is cheap and abundant in London, and prices are not half what they are in new countries, which are flourishing, and where money is scarce. Double the amount of money in the world, and you double prices. Double its amount in any one country, and in many instances you would diminish prices.— Wheat and corn, and negroes, and manufactured articles, would sell no higher in Virginia, if her currency were quadrupled, for she would have her prices determined for those articles, by the markets of the world. Lands fitted for mere grain producing would sell no higher, for their value would be determined by the amount of money their crops would fetch in foreign markets, and be not at all affected by the amount of money in Virginia, for Virginia makes more grain than she can consume, and foreign markets regulate its price. City lots and houses would rise in value, but even in them the prices would be somewhat regulated by the prices of the world, for men will sooner quit their country than give inordinate prices for houses to live in. We never could account for the common error and folly of political economists, in supposing that a local increase of currency, would be followed by a corresponding increase of prices. If it were true, then the balance of trade would be of no advantage, but it is foolishly false.

The balance of trade, the accumulation and increase of money, having no determinate influence on prices, in many cases diminishing them, in a few increasing them, what is to become of the accession to the currency, for which the business of the community has no use or demand? Men will not let their money lie idle. It cannot be employed by themselves, or by those who borrow it, in existing pursuits. They are all filled up. The consequence is, that new pursuits arise. An agricultural country becomes a commercial and manufacturing one, and thus four or five times the money is required for its transactions. Ships and factories are built, and thousands of laborers and artisans are introduced for the purpose. Then it becomes necessary to build houses, to construct roads, and to make canals. Now there is use for the increase of money, occasioned by the favorable balance of trade; and as one dollar in currency represents some twenty in property, every dollar imported in excess over dollars exported, will occasion an increase of local and national wealth of twenty dollars. The man who saves a thousand dollars of his income is only a thousand dollars richer,

F

but the nation that saves a thousand dollars adds twenty thousand to its wealth. We are no cosmopolite philanthropists, and will not stop to enquire the effects on the wealth of the world, but we undertake to say, that the local advantages of the balance of trade have been grossly underrated by its warmest advocates. Political economists have ever been the astutest, but most narrow-minded and least comprehensive of men.

Whilst on this subject we will remark, that so far as we have examined their works, they confound the simplest rules of logic. They treat of political economy as a mere physical science, of man as a mere machine, impelled by mechanical forces, and determine the results of all national policy and industrial avocations by measurements of time, distance, cost of transportation, capacity of soil, climate, &c. Now the effect of an exclusive policy on a people highly intellectual, having many wants, moral, mental and physical, in a Northern clime, with a sterile soil, is to stimulate that people to the exertion of mind and body, and to make them produce in a small compass all that human skill, industry and ingenuity can procure. In such a country, as in the little republics of Greece, under an exclusive policy, the wisdom of a world must concentrate, else their wants, moral, physical and intellectual, will be unsupplied. On the other hand, a people who are supplied by commerce with all that their natures require are lured and enticed to betake themselves to some simple operation, such as agriculture, and thus become poor, half-civilized and ignorant. We appeal to history to attest the universal truth of our theory. Trade never did civilize a people; never failed to degrade them, unless they supplied the manufactured articles. On another occasion we may show how this confounding of the moral with the physical, renders worthless all the speculations of the economists.

As further proof and illustration of our theory, as to the balance of trade, we cite the following examples:—A country continually declining in wealth, would have each day less use for a circulating medium, and would export a part of it. On the other hand, a country improving in wealth and population, must continually increase her medium of exchange. The balance of trade is, therefore, always against the declining country, and in favor of the improving one. It remains only to show, that this diminution of currency may be a *cause* of decline, and its increase a cause of improvement. The importation of agricultural instruments into a country with a rich soil, and plenty of inhabitants, but without those instruments, would increase its wealth a thousand fold. Now, money is not only necessary to set agriculture in operation, but far more necessary in all other industrial pursuits. Therefore, the increase of money, like the increase of tools of farming, sets men to work in a thousand ways, in which they could not engage without such increase. The Negroes, the Indians, the Mexicans and Lazzaroni of Naples, would not be benefited by the increase of currency, by bank expansions, and by a favorable balance of trade, but all people who are ripe and prepared for new enterprises, will be immensely benefited by such increase and expansion.

Banks have become so important a part of our institutions, and exercise so controlling an influence on the wealth and well being of individuals and of States, that any treatise on social science would be imperfect, that omitted to notice them.

Their importance is greatly increased in this country by the existence almost every where of restraining laws, which prohibit and punish private banking, or the issue of private paper, payable to bearer. Private credit being, we think, very properly restricted in this way, it becomes the duty of the State to supply its place as fairly and equally as practicable by bank credit, in the form of bank notes. In Virginia especially, the note holders have been more than compensated for the deprivation of this form of private credit, by the greater security afforded through means of corporate banks.

Whether the effect of unrestricted free banking would be permanently to flood the country with worthless paper, or by re-action and loss of confidence in all such paper, to bring it back to a specie currency, is a question we will not undertake to solve. We are inclined to believe a currency solely metallic would be the consequence. Such a currency is wholly unfitted to the wants and usages of modern society.

The Virginia system of banking, with mother banks and branches, has operated well so far as security to note holders, and integrity of administration are concerned. We have no doubt the system, with slight modifications, will be continued. In a growing and improving State, its capacity for expansion is one of its greatest recommendations. It would be well, within certain limits, that the Legislature should permit the present banks, at any time, to increase their capitals, and to establish branches at such points, and with such capital, as they please—giving them the further power to wind up such branches when they pleased. We might thus obtain a currency capable of expanding and contracting with the wants and exigencies of trade. Now, we have a fixed and stationary amount of currency, with a population rapidly increasing in wealth and numbers. In the last five years the increase of prices, occasioned by the mines of California and Australia, and the growth and increase of our towns, internal improvements, &c., has doubled the moneyed price of the property of Virginia. Yet in that five years a very small addition has been made to our banking capital. Either that capital was entirely too great five years ago, or

it is now much too small, and is cramping industry, energy and enterprise, and preventing growth
and development.

Some political economists contend that the
increase of currency in a country, metallic or
paper, after the existing demands of trade are
satisfied, increases all prices, but does not add
to national wealth. Others restrict and qualify
the proposition, and maintain that such increase
only enhances the prices of immoveable articles,
whose value is not determined by the markets of
the world. Their doctrines are equally false. As
a permanent and normal fact, the prices of lands,
labor and city lots, are no more affected by a redundant currency than those of wheat, cotton
and tobacco. Rich men, with plenty of money,
do not pay more for what they buy than the poor,
but less. In like manner, rich communities and
cities, like New York and London, affording a
better market, pay less for what they buy and
sell cheaper than poorer places. New banks, like
young merchants, have to buy their experience.
They give too much credit, encourage speculation and visionary unprofitable enterprises,
and thus inflate the prices of every thing around
them for a time. Failures occur, re-action takes
place, they become over cautious, and depress
prices as far below the proper standard, as they
had inflated above it. After awhile they learn

to conduct business properly, and then prices assume a proper and safe level.

Two years more must transpire before the Legislature can convene, re-charter the present banks, or establish a new system, and get that system, or additional branches of the present system, into operation. That the State will suffer greatly from this delay we think there can be little doubt.

A banking system, such as we suggest, would wield much power, and constitute a most important governmental institution. Its influence would be conservative, and its administration probably fair, equal and impartial. The number of mother banks would secure enough of competition, and their interests would induce them to establish branches, when and where only they would be profitable. The stockholders of banks are generally men of much experience and knowledge in business, cautious and conservative in their dealings, and opposed to speculations. They are men living on their incomes, whose fortunes are made, and who have no temptations to incur risk. The control of the amount of currency might be safely left in their hands, for either too great expansions or contractions would injure them.— Universal suffrage has given to the 'progressive element in society, the poor, the young, and the enterprising, so much power, that this conservative balance would not be amiss.

The prices of land, and the wages of labor, are regulated and fixed generally by the prices of the products of land and labor, and not at all influenced by the scarcity or abundance of money.

The safe and legitimate influence of expansion, or increase of currency, by stimulating enterprises that are profitable, is what no one complains of. This brings us to consider the doctrine which we maintained in our chapter on the Balance of Trade,—That the increase of currency, when it is merely local or national, will not inflate prices, but if it gives rise to new pursuits of industry and new investments of capital which are profitable, that then each thousand dollars added to the currency of a country will add at least twenty thousand to its wealth. In this we assume that each dollar in a community is represented by twenty dollars of property. Now, no people are ready for an increase of their currency, until they are also ready so to increase their population, and to vary and add to their trade and pursuits, as to have twenty times as much additional capital in property as additional currency. In new countries we see instances every day where the value of property is added to twenty fold, in a single year. In an old country the same thing will occur, provided accessions to the currency occasion new and profitable pursuits and enterprises sufficient permanently to absorb and employ such accessions.

The banks of this State, if they can profitably double their issues, can only do so by increasing existing trade and business, or by originating measures that will result in an increase of the wealth of the State twenty fold the increase of their issues. Every people ought to have among them as much money as can be profitably employed, because each additional dollar so employed adds ere long twenty to State wealth. If a million of dollars were permanently taken away from the currency of a country, it must either change its pursuits and engage in modes of industry requiring less capital in money; or if it continues its then existing trade and pursuits, it must lessen their amount in proportion to the diminution of the currency. This only could be effected by diminishing the property of the country twenty millions—that is, on the assumption that twenty millions of property require for its proper administration, sales and transfers, one million of money. As we have before contended, an increase of a million in currency, to render that increase permanent and profitable, must be followed by a corresponding increase in trade, and that this increase of trade could only occur under ordinary circumstances, when there was an increase of twenty millions in the property of the country, to require such trade.

It can make no difference whether the increase of currency be occasioned by bank expansions or the importation of specie. If the specie be not needed, it will be exported; if the paper be not required, it will return on the banks. If either continue in circulation, it is because the country is increasing, or has increased its property, (of other kinds than money,) twenty fold the increase of currency. The increase of currency must neither entirely precede nor follow the increase of business. It should occur as soon and as fast as prudent, sensible, and honest men are willing to borrow and employ it. *Experienced* bank officers and stockholders will be the best judges of when and where to increase or diminish the currency. We conclude that if Virginia be ready for an increase of her currency in paper or coin, she is ready for twenty times as much increase of her property, and that such increase cannot be permanently made in her currency without producing such increase in her property. We believe she is now ready for a very large increase of currency, provided such increase be made by judicious laws, at proper points in the State.— Without it, industry must remain hampered, and growth and development be prevented.

The doctrine that banks necessarily occasion speculation and improvidence is untrue. Loans of coin are used as improvidently as loans of paper. The stockholders, if there were no banks, would loan their money in specie; now through the banks they loan it in paper.

The banks of Virginia, if they err at all, err on the safe side, that of extreme caution in making loans. But they aid the poor, the young and enterprising, by lending small sums on short dates to mechanics, merchants, manufacturers, &c. Private individuals lend their money in large sums, on long credits, to farmers and other wealthy capitalists. Money lent by banks, usually exercises a better influence on the well being and progress of society than money loaned by individuals. All Southern cities had excess of bank capital twenty years ago, but this excess neither produced speculation nor enhanced the price of town lots.

CHAPTER XI.

Nothing has more perplexed political economists and mankind at large, than the subject of usury. That it was right, proper, and laudable for every man to get the highest market price for the use of his money, as for the use of every other article, was an obvious deduction from all the axioms of the economists. The instincts and common sense of mankind, whilst admitting the premises, stubbornly denied the unavoidable conclusion. Convicted in argument, but not convinced, they still fought on. In truth, the error lay in the premises, in the axioms and first principles of political economy. That systematic selfishness that inculcates the moral duty to let every man take care of himself and his own selfish interest, that advises each to use his wits, his prudence, and his providence, to get the better of those who have less wit, prudence and providence, to make the best bargains one can, and that a thing is worth what it will bring, is false and rotten to the core. It bears no sound fruit, brings forth no good morality. "Laissez nous faire," and "Caveat Emptor," (the latter the maxim of the common law,) justify usury, encourage the weak to oppress the strong, and would justify swindling and theft, if fully carried out into practice. But it is not safe or prudent to swindle or steal; one incurs the penalties of the law; and it is not politic, for one scares off customers and subjects. The man who makes good shaving bargains, will in the long run grow rich; the swindler and the thief never do. Mankind have ever detested the extortionate usurer who takes advantage of distress and misfortune to increase his profits, more than a Robin Hood who robs the rich to relieve the poor. There is always at bottom some sound moral reason for the prejudices of mankind. Analyze their motives, their feelings and sentiments closely. The man who spends a life in dealing hardly and harshly with his fellow men, is a much worse and meaner man than the highway robber. The latter is chivalrous, and where there is chivalry there will be occasional generosity.

The law should protect men, as well from the assaults of superior wit as from those of superior bodily strength. Men's inequalities of wit, prudence, and providence, differ in nothing so much, as in their capacity to deal in and take care of money. This creates the necessity for laws against usury. Under occasional circumstances, a heavy rate of interest is morally right, but it is generally wrong, and laws are passed for ordinary and not extraordinar occasions.

We do not think badly of our fellow men, but badly of their philosophy. Their kind feelings, impulses, and sentiments, get the better of their principles, and they are continually doing good and preaching evil.

If men were no better than political economy would make them, the world would be a Pandemonium.

The Bible fortunately is a more common book than Adam Smith. Its influences are exerted over the hearts and conduct of thousands who never enter a church. "The still small voice of conscience" oft brings back the mother's image, and the mother's divine precepts, "Love thy neighbor as thyself," "Do unto others as you would that they should do unto you."

As we pursue this investigation, we become daily more disposed to adopt the theory of Robespiere, "that political economy and infidelity are one and the same." It was the Devil rebuking sin; and well he might, for infidel France sinned to such an excess as to tire the Devil of his own work.

> ———"Even the very Devil
> On this occasion his own work abhorred,
> So surfeited with the infernal revel;
> Though he himself had sharpened every sword,
> It almost quenched his innate thirst of evil."

CHAPTER XII.

Towns and villages are breaks that arrest and prevent the exhausting drain of agriculture, aided by rivers and roads. They consume the crops of the neighborhood, its wood and timber, and thus not only furnish a home market, but manures to replenish the lands. They afford respectable occupations, in the mechanic' arts, commerce, manufactures, and the professions, for the energetic young men of the neighborhood. They sustain good schools, which a sparse country neighborhood never can. They furnish places and opportunities for association and rational enjoyment to the neighborhood around. They support good ministers and churches, and thus furnish religious consolation and instruction to many who have not the means to visit distant places of worship.— Rivers and roads, without towns, are mere facilities offered to agriculture- to carry off the crops, to exhaust the soil, and to remove the inhabitants, rich and poor. This was strikingly exemplified in Virginia a few years ago. The people on the rich lands, on navigable rivers, were a few absentees, without villages, towns, mechanic arts, churches or schools. They made money at home, and the rivers tempted them to spend it abroad. They would not send their grain to the little towns at the head of tide water, because New York and Boston were equally convenient, and better markets to buy and sell in. Our towns were robbed of the trade of their neighbors below by the rivers, and there were no roads to bring them trade from above. The poor region just above the head of tide-water, was becoming rich from necessity. They were obliged to have villages, mechanic arts, and manufactures at home. They had no roads or rivers, and were cut off from the blessings of free trade. Their villages contained good schools and churches, and thus compressed within a small compass the advantages of society and civilization. Most of these villages will be ruined by the roads we are constructing to the West. There will be no use for them when farmers can sell their crops and get their supplies on better terms from the large towns. The agricultural portion of the West will be injured by our system of improvements. Luckily for the West, her varied and rich mineral resources, and her water-power, will occasion mining and manufactures to be carried on, towns to arise, and home markets to be offered to the farmer. This will be the situation of the West generally, but in sections where there are neither mines nor water-power, the country will be impoverished by the improvements.

An overgrown State, like an overgrown man, is not generally equal in wisdom or strength to one of moderate size. The most distinguished, learned and wealthy States of ancient and modern times, have had small dominions and small populations. They have been obliged, in order to secure their independence, to prosecute every art, science, trade and avocation belonging to civilized life. Thus a few came to understand and practice what many performed in large and cumbrous States. A small nationality and dense population, not cursed by free trade, necessarily produces an intense civilization, provided the nation be of a race that needs and loves civilization.

The effect of free trade and extended dominions, is to remove from most individuals and sections the necessity to acquire and practice the arts of life that require skill and learning, and thus to dilute and degrade civilization.

But separate nationality is a mere form, not a reality, when free trade furnishes what the nation should produce at home.

The cities in the South, on tide-water, will grow rapidly, as soon as roads enough penetrate the West. People from the interior, will sell their grain and buy their manufactures, groceries and other goods, from those cities. Few, very few, will change from the cars to vessels, carry their grain North, and buy their supplies there. Around all these Southern cities the country will become rich. It will be dotted with gardens, orchards and villas. Large cities, like New York and London, are great curses, because they impoverish a world to enrich a neighborhood. Numerous small towns are great blessings, because they prevent the evil effects of centralization of trade, retain wealth and population at home, and diffuse happiness and intelligence, by begetting variety of pursuits, supporting schools, colleges and religious institutions, and affording the means of pleasant and frequent association.

Each Southern State may condense within its boundaries all the elements of separate independent nationality. Civilization is imperfect and incomplete until this state of things arises. Each State must not only have within itself good lawyers, doctors and farmers, but able statesmen, learned philosophers, distinguished artists, skilful mechanics, great authors, and every institution and pursuit that pertain to high civilization. Railroads almost invariably increase national wealth to an amount greatly exceeding the cost of their construction. In countries purely agricultural, the increase of wealth which they occasion, and the diminution of wealth which, when properly located, they prevent, is almost incalcu-

lable. All the money spent in the constructio
of the road is money saved, for in merely agricul
tural countries all money not spent in living i
carried off in some way from the country. But
besides the addition of the road itself, to th
wealth of such a country, the increase of capita
in houses, the enhanced value of lots and lands
&c., at the town where they terminate, usuall
greatly exceeds the [cost of the road. Ever
road that has been constructed from any of- ou
seaboard Atlantic cities, has produced this effect
They have occasioned already an increase in th
value of property in those cities far greater thar
the cost of their construction. Whilst their erec
tion is going on, they afford respectable and pro
fitable employment to thousands near their track
They also afford an excellent market to the far
mer for his wood and timber, and many othei
things that were before unsaleable. From thes
various considerations, it would seem to follow
at first view, that they should be constructed a
State expense. Especially, since it is desirabl
that public roads should not be the subjects o
monopoly.

The gross and grievous inequalities in the bur
den of taxation, and the resulting benefits o
roads constructed at public expense, is a stron
consideration against such mode of construction
Men living a distance from the roads derive n

advantages from them, yet must pay equally for building; men owning valuable stores, taverns, &c., in the interior, near where a road passes, are often made to pay for improvements that will render their property valueless. Whilst the owners of vacant lots at the termini, who have scarce paid any of the tax that built the road, make often immense fortunes by the increase occasioned in the value of their lots.

On the other hand, when the public spirited and patriotic, the young, the enterprising and the poor, erect public improvements, the rich old fogies laugh at their enterprise, refuse to aid to the amount of a cent, and Pharisaically congratulate themselves on their virtue, prudence and good sense, in securing, by the situation of their property, the larger portion of the profits arising from such schemes, if successful, without incurring any risk or a cent of cost.

The towns where they terminate might erect them and make a profit by doing so. But the owners of houses, merchandise and money would pay for them, and the owners of vacant lots reap most of the profits.

We will not undertake to determine how, or at whose cost, public improvement should be constructed. We think it would be best to lay down no general rule, but for the Legislature to act on each application, according to the necessity, char-

acter and probable profits and advantages of the
proposed work.

Eastern Virginians often complain that they
are taxed to build roads for the West. Roads
piercing an agricultural interior, and terminating
at towns, at or near the ocean, usually impoverish
the interior and create immense wealth in the
seaboard towns, and in the country near them.

If such should be, and to a great extent it no
doubt will be, the result of our roads, then Western Virginia might with great propriety complain that she was made "to pay for a stick to
break her own head."

Eastern Virginia is exceedingly conservative.
She opposes all innovations, and sticks to mud
roads as pertinaciously as many of her old gentry did to fairtops, shorts and kneebuckles. But
she must give way at last, for she is proud and
highly civilized. Rapid intercommunication is the
distinguishing feature. of modern progress. 'Tis
part and parcel of the civilization of our times.
Daily mails, telegraphs and railroads are becoming necessaries of life. Fashion is omnipotent,
and these things are exceedingly useful, and "all
the rage" to boot. 'Tis easy to be a prophet in
Eastern Virginia. She invents nothing, but slowly
and reluctantly follows in the wake of less digni-
fied, more fickle, and progressive regions. Go to
England or the North, and you can foretell our

condition ten years hence, as certainly as you can tell this season in Paris the fashion of ladies' bonnets next season in America. We will monopolise the advantages of the system we oppose, for not more naturally and certainly do rivers bring detritus and alluvium from the mountains, to lodge them at their mouths and deltas, than do railroads bring the wealth of the interior to enrich the towns and country on the seaboard.

CHAPTER XIII.

EDUCATION.

The abolitionists taunt us with the ignorance of our poor white citizens. This is a stigma on the South that should be wiped out. Half of the people of the South, or nearly so, are blacks. We have only to educate the other half. At the North, they educate all. Our Southern free-trade philosophy, our favorite maxim, " every man for himself," has been the cause of the neglect of popular education. The civilized world differ from us and censure us. They say it is the first duty of government to provide for the education of all its citizens. Despotic Prussia compels parents to send their children to schools supported at public expense. All are educated and well educated. As our's is a government of the people, no where is education so necessary. The poor, too, ask no charity, when they demand universal education. They constitute our militia and our police. They protect men in possession of property, as in other countries; and do much more, they secure men in possession of a kind of property which they could not hold a day but for the supervision and protection of the poor. This very property has rendered the South merely agricultural, made population too sparse for neighborhood schools, prevented variety of pursuits, and thus cut the poor off as well from the means of living, as from the means of education.

Universal suffrage will soon attempt to remedy these evils. But rashness and precipitancy may occasion failure and bring about despondency. We are not yet prepared to educate all. Free schools should at once be established in all neighborhoods where a sufficient number of scholars can be collected in one school. Parents should be compelled to send their children to school. The obligation on the part of government, to educate the people, carries with it the indubitable right to employ all the means necessary to attain that end. But the duty of government does not end with educating the people. As far as is practicable, it should open to them avenues of employment in which they may use what they have learned. The system of internal improvements now carried on in the South, will directly and indirectly, quite suffice to attain this end, so far as government can aid properly in such an object. Government may do too much for the people, or it may do too little. We have committed the latter error.

The mail and the newspaper-press might be employed, as cheap and efficient agents, in teaching the masses. No family in the Union is so dull, stupid and indifferent, as not to be curious about the news of the day. Cotemporaneous history is the most interesting and important part of history. That is to be had alone from newspapers. But newspapers contain on all subjects the most recent discoveries, and the most valuable information.

A large weekly newspaper might be furnished to every poor family in the State, at less than a dollar a family. If there were not a teacher within fifty miles, some member of each family would learn to read, first to get at the neighborhood news and scandals, the deaths, and marriages, and murders. Gradually they would understand and become interested in the proceedings of our government, and the news from foreign countries. The meanest newspaper in the country is worth all the libraries in Christendom. It is desirable to know what the ancients did, but it is necessary to know what our neighbors and fellow country-men are doing.

Our system of improvements, manufactures, the mechanic arts, the building up of our cities, commerce, and education should go hand in hand. We ought not to attempt too much at once. 'Tis time we were attempting something. We ought, like the Athenians, to be the best educated people in the world. When we employ all our whites in the mechanic arts, in commerce, in professions, &c., and confine the negroes to farm-work, and coarse mechanical operations, we shall be in a fair way to attain this result. The abolition movement is a harmless humbug, confined to a handful of fanatics, but the feeling of antipathy to negroes, the hatred of race, and the disposition to expel them from the country is daily increasing, North and South. Two causes are in active operation to fan and increase this hostility to the negro race. The one, the neglect to educate and provide means of employment for the poor whites in the South, who are thereby led to believe that the existence of negroes amongst us is ruin to them. The other, the theory of the Types of Mankind, which cuts off the negro from human brotherhood, and justifies the brutal and the miserly in treating him as a vicious brute. Educate all Southern whites, employ them, not as cooks, lacqueys, ploughmen, and menials, but as independent freemen should be employed, and let negroes be strictly tied down to such callings as are unbecoming white men, and peace would be established between blacks and whites. The whites would find themselves elevated by the existence of negroes amongst us. Like the Roman citizen, the Southern white man would become a noble and a privileged character, and he would then like negroes and slavery, because his high position would be due to them. Poor people can see things as well as rich people. We can't hide the facts from them. It is always better openly, honestly, and fearlessly to meet danger, than to fly from or avoid it. The last words we will utter on this subject are,—The path of safety is the path of duty! Educate the people, no matter what it may cost!

CHAPTER XIV.

EXCLUSIVE AGRICULTURE.

Writing as we do, with the hope of suggesting some things useful to the South, we deem the subject of agriculture, their favorite and almost sole pursuit, one worthy of separate consideration, especially as it is intimately connected with the doctrines of free trade. Agriculture can never be the exclusive pursuit of a civilized people, unless by free trade, all other wants than those of food, are supplied from abroad. Man naturally gives a preference to agriculture over all other avocations, because it is the most simple and the most independent. This preference is greatly increased when the climate and soil are adapted to its pursuit. Such is the case in the Southern States, with the additional inducement in its favor, that the laboring class, the negroes, are admirably fitted for farming, and too ignorant and dull for any of the finer processes of the mechanic arts. Hence the South has become almost exclusively agricultural, and hence, also, she has ever been the advocate of free trade, which supplies the many wants that agriculture leaves unsupplied.

The usual and familiar arguments in favor of this policy are, that it is cheaper to buy abroad good manufactured articles in exchange for agricultural products, than to buy them at home, where more indifferent articles would be obtained for a larger amount of agricultural products.

And again, that we, having no skill or spare moneyed capital, but possessing a rich soil, fine climate, and suitable labor for farming, should follow farming, whilst other nations, without these advantages, but having a large moneyed capital, and great artistic and mechanical skill, should produce manufactured articles, and exchange them for our grain and other . products. that thus both we and they would be benefited. The argument is specious, but as false as it is specious.

If an agricultural people were found without any manufactures, by a manufacturing one, the effect of free trade would be to prevent the invention and practice of all the mechanic arts, for " necessity is the mother of invention," and such trade would remove the necessity of home manufactures. But, in truth, there never was a people, however savage, without some knowledge of manufactures and the mechanic arts. When that knowledge, as in the instances of Africans and Indians, is very slight, and the processes of course very tedious, laborious, and inefficient, the im-

mediate effect of contact with a civilized nation
by trade, is to extinguish the little knowledge
they have, and to divert them to fishing, hunting,
searching for gold and similar pursuits, which
savages can practice almost as well as civilized
men. The African ceases to smelt iron when he
finds a day's work in hunting for slaves, iron or
gold, will purchase more and better instruments
than he could make in a week, and the Indian
pursues trapping, and hunting, and fishing, exclusively, when he can exchange his game, his
furs and fish, for blankets, guns, powder and
whiskey, with the American. Thus does free trade
prevent the growth of civilization and depress
and destroy it, by removing the necessity that
alone can beget it. Its effects on agricultural
countries, however civilized, are precisely similar
in character to those on savages. Necessity compels people in poor regions, to cultivate commerce
and the mechanic arts, and for that purpose to
build ships and cities. They soon acquire skill
in manufactures, and all the advantages necessary
to produce them with cheapness and facility.
The agricultural people with whom they trade,
have been bred to exclusive farming, by the sim-
plicity of its operations, its independence of life,
and the fertility of their soil. If cut off like
China was, and Japan yet is, from the rest of the
civilized world, they would have to practise at

home all the arts, trades and professions of civilized life, in order to supply the wants of civilized beings. But trade will supply everything they need, except the products of the soil. As they are unskilled in mechanic arts, have few towns, little accumulated capital, and a sparse population, they produce, with great labor and expense, all manufactured articles. To them it is cheaper, at present, to exchange their crops for manufactures than to make them. They begin the exchange, and each day the necessity increases for continuing it, for each day they learn to rely more and more on others to produce articles, some of which they formerly manufactured,—and their ignorance of all, save agriculture, is thus daily increasing. It is cheaper for a man, little skilled in mechanics, to buy his plough and wagon by the exchange of agricultural products, than awkwardly, clumsily and tediously to manufacture them of bad quality with his own hands. Yet, if this same man will become a skilful mechanic, he will be able to procure four times as much agricultural products for his labor, as he can now secure with his own hands. His labor too, will be of a lighter, less exposed, more social character, and far more improving to his mind. What is true of the individual, is true as to a nation, the people who buy their manufactures abroad, labor four times as hard, and as long, to

produce them, as if they made them at home.
In the case of the nation, this exclusive agriculture begets a sparse and poor population; sparse,
because no more people can be employed, than
are sufficient to cultivate the land,—poor, because their labor, though harder and more exposed, produces in the aggregate about one-fourth
what the same amount of lighter labor would, in
a purely mechanical and manufacturing country.
Density of population doubles and quadruples
the value of labor and of property, because it furnishes the opportunity for association and division of labor, and the division of charges and expenses. When one man has to bear the expense
of a school, a church, a mill, a store, a smith's
shop, &c., he is very apt to let his family go without religion and education, and his farm without
many of the necessaries and conveniences that
properly appertain to it. Where a few have to
bear these expenses, the burden on each is very
heavy, but where, as in manufacturing countries,
with a dense population and many villages, these
expenses are sub-divided among many, the burden is light to each,—so that their property and
their labor is vastly more available and valuable.

The sparsely settled agricultural country makes
by its pursuits, one-fourth what the manufacturing country does, and the money that it makes is
probably, in general, if spent at home, capable

of purchasing one-half only of the pleasures, comforts and luxuries of life that the same amount of money would in countries engaged in other pursuits. The pleasures of society are seldom indulged in, or if indulged in, at much expense of time and inconvenience, in merely farming countries, where people live at considerable distance from each other. There is no occasion for towns or cities, and not enough of the rich to support places of recreation and amusement. The rich are, therefore, all absentees. Some go off for pleasure, some to religious conventions and associations, some for education, and those who remain at home, do so not to spend money and improve the country, but to save it, in order that they too may hereafter visit other regions. The latter class are no less absentees, in effect, than the former classes. The consumption abroad, of the crops made at home would, in two centuries, blast the prosperity of any country, by robbing it of the manures which nature intended for it. Where there are many manufacturing villages they furnish a constant supply of manure to the country around. The manure made from the farmer's crop, consumed in those villages, is returned to his soil, mixed with a thousand other fertilizing ingredients from the streets, sewers, and factories of the town. Thus only can agriculture flourish, and a soil be kept permanently rich.

Few, very few men, will acquire education, or confer it on their children, unless some pecuniary advantage is to result from it. The mass of population in farming countries are field hands. They require no education whatever, even if their wages would procure it. The managers or overseers need but little, for much as agricultural chemistry and scientific farming are talked about, everybody's instinctive common sense and judgment teaches, that they are part of the humbugs of the day. No person would employ an overseer who was learned in the natural sciences. Botany, geology, chemistry, mineralogy, and natural history, do very well for the closet philosopher, but would be dangerous attainments in an overseer. The farmers of Judea, Egypt, Greece and Rome, two and four thousand years ago, were better than ours. Farming rapidly declined in Rome, so soon as Cato and others attempted to make it a science. The most potent qualities of soils and atmospheres evade all analysis. No difference is found in the death-dealing air of the Pontine Marshes, and the pure atmosphere of the Appenines. When fever, plague, or cholera rage in New Orleans, the minutest analysis can detect nothing in the air that was not there before, nothing which does not exist in it in the healthiest regions. Each adjoining acre of land may produce wine or tobacco of very different qualities,

yet no chemist can tell the why. Philosophy cannot prevent the weevil, the rust, or the joint
worm.

Chemists undertake to analyze exactly a grain
of wheat, and to determine accurately and precisely its component parts. Now, when they can
make a grain of wheat, that will vegetate and
grow and bear fruit, we will believe in agricultural chemistry. Till then, we shall contend that
there is something too minute and recondite in
vegetable life for mortal ken to read, and will
throw their physic to the dogs.

The great secrets of animal and vegetable life,
and of their health, growth and decay, are in a
great measure hidden from human search. Philosophy makes no advances in this direction. Galen
and Hippocrates were as good physicians as the
latest graduate of Edinburgh, and Cato as good
a farmer as Mr. Newton. "A Paul may plant,
and an Apollos water, but God alone can give
the increase."

Farming is the recreation of great men, the
proper pursuit of dull men. And the dull are the
most successful, because they imitate, observe,
and never experiment. Washington and Cincin-
natus farmed for amusement, George the Third
and Sancho Panza, because it was their appropriate avocation. Ambitious men sometimes, to
hide their designs, and allay suspicion, rear game

cocks, or "cultivate peas and philosophy." But farmers have no use for learning, and a farming country would not be a learned one if books grew on trees, and "reading and writing came by nature."

The population as it increases must emigrate, for the want of variety of pursuits, and more avenues of employment. A manufacturing State, if it can find agricultural people weak enough to trade with them, may sustain an enlightened population indefinite in numbers, for the more dense the population, the better it is adapted for mechanical and manufacturing pursuits. Internal improvements, like schools and colleges, cannot be well sustained in farming States, because the people are too few and too poor to make or support them.

Holland and Massachusetts are two of the richest, happiest, and most highly civilized States in the world, because they farm very little, but are engaged in more profitable and enlightened pursuits. The soil of Massachusetts is very poor, and that of Holland not adapted to grain. Ireland, the East and West Indies, and our Southern States, are poor and ignorant countries with rich soils. They farm altogether, and their rich and enterprising and ambitious men desert them for pleasure, promotion, or employment, in lands less favored by nature, but improved by man.

The South must vary and multiply her pursuits, consume her crops at home, keep her people at home, increase her population, build up
cities, towns and villages, establish more schools
and colleges, educate the poor, construct internal improvements, carry on her own commerce,
and carry on that if possible with more Southern
regions : for the North, whether in Europe or
here, will manufacture for, cheat her, and keep
her dependent. She would manufacture for the
far South, and get thus the same profits and advantages that are now extracted from her by the
North. Do these things and she will be rich,
enlightened and independent, neglect them and
she will become poor, weak and contemptible.
Her State Rights doctrines will be derided, and
her abstractions scoffed at.

In connection with this subject, we will venture
a suggestion to the South, (for we may not presume to advise,) as to the intellectual progress
and improvement which the mechanic arts, and
those arts alone open to human study, investigation and invention. We have just stated that
the world has not improved in the last two thousand, probably four thousand years, in the science
or practice of medicine, or agriculture; we now
add that it has all this while been retrograding
in all else save the physical sciences and the
mechanic arts. Rome imitated and fell short of

Greece, in all the departments of moral philosophy, in pure metaphysics, in poetry, in architecture, in sculpture, in oratory, in the drama, and in painting, and we to-day imitate Rome. It is idle to talk of progress, when we look two thousand years back for models of perfection. So vast was Grecian superiority in art above ours, that it is a common theory, that they possessed an ideal to guide them, which has been lost, and which loss is irreparable. The ancients understood the art, practice and science of government better than we. There was more intelligence, more energy, more learning, more happiness, more people, and more wealth, around the Levant, and in its islands, in the days of Herodotus, than are now to be found in all Europe.

The only progress or advancement visible to the eye, is that brought about by the mechanic arts, aided by physical science. Chemistry and natural philosophy would have remained dead letters, had not the mechanic stepped in to construct the cannon and the gun, the compass, the steam engine, and the electric wire. Looking back through the vista of ages, the noblest and oldest monuments of human intellect and human energy are the works of the mechanic. Long ere the Muse lisped in liquid and melodious numbers, long before the buskined Drama trod the stage, long before the Historian in stately march arrayed the dim and distant past, the Mechanic had built pyramids, and walls, and cities, and temples, that have defied the lapse and corrosion of time. We are at a loss which most to admire, the first efforts of his genius, his energy and skill, as daily developed at Nineveh, in Egypt, in Rome, and in Greece, or his latest achievements in his steamships, railroads, immense factories, and time and distance destroying telegraph. He looks into heaven with his telescope, he is omnipresent with his telegraph, may he not reach heaven in some aerial car. *Sic itur ad astra!* Let the ambitious South cultivate, not spurn the mechanic arts.

CHAPTER XV.

If the Socialists had done no other good, they would be entitled to the gratitude of mankind for displaying in a strong light the advantages of the association of labor. Adam Smith, in his elaborate treatise on the Division of Labor, nearly stumbled on the same truth. But the division of labor is a curse to the laborer, without the association of labor. Division makes labor ten times more efficient, but by confining each workman to some simple, monotonous employment, it makes him a mere automaton, and an easy prey to the capitalist. The association of labor, like all associations, requires a head or ruler, and that head or ruler will become a cheat and a tyrant, unless his interests are identified with the interests of the laborer. In a large factory, in free society, there is division of labor, and association too, but association and division for the benefit of the employer and to the detriment of the laborer. On a large farm, whatever advances the health, happiness and morals of the negroes, renders them more prolific and valuable to their master. It is his interest to pay them high wages in way of support, and he can afford to do so, because association renders the labor of each slave five times as productive and efficient as it would be, were the slaves working separately. One man could not enclose an acre of land, cultivate it, send his crops to market, do his own cooking, washing and mending. One man may live as a prowling beast of prey, but not as a civilized being. One hundred human beings, men, women and children, associated, will cultivate ten acres of land each, enclose it, and carry on every other operation of civilized life. Labor becomes at least twenty times as productive when a hundred associate, as when one acts alone. The same is as true in other pursuits as in farming. But in free society, the employer robs the laborer, and he is no better off than the prowling savage, although he might live in splendor if he got a fair proportion of the proceeds of his own labor.

We have endeavored to show, heretofore, that the negro slave, considering his indolence and unskilfulness, often gets his fair share, and sometimes more than his share, of the profits of the farm, and is exempted, besides, from the harassing cares and anxieties of the free laborer. Grant, however, that the negro does not receive adequate wages from his master, yet all admit that in the aggregate the negroes get better wages than free laborers; therefore, it follows that, with all its imperfections, slave society is the best form of society yet devised for the masses. When Socialists and Abolitionists, by full and fair experiments, exhibit a better, it will be time to agitate the subject of abolition.

The industrial products of black slave labor have been far greater and more useful to mankind, than those of the same amount of any other labor. In a very short period, the South and South-west have been settled, cleared, fenced in, and put in cultivation, by what were, a century ago, a handful of masters and slaves. This region now feeds and clothes a great part of mankind; but free trade cheats them of the profits of their labor. In the vast amount of our industrial products, we see the advantages of association—in our comparative poverty, the evils of free trade.

CHAPTER XVI.

THE FREE LABORER'S CARES AND ANXIETIES.

We think we have shown in the preceding chapter, not only that the physical condition of the free laborer is worse than that of the slave, but that its evils are intolerable. It is admitted and is proved to be so by the almost unanimous authority of rich and poor, learned and ignorant, living in the midst of free society. What is the mental condition of the free laborer? Is he exempt from the cares that beset wealth and power, and plant thorns in the path of royalty?

Poor men have families as well as the rich, and they love those families more than rich men, because they have little else to love. The smiles of their wives and the prattle of their children, when they return from labor at night, compensate, in some degree, for the want of those luxuries which greet the rich, but which render them less keenly alive to the pleasures of domestic affection. Their love is divided between their possessions and their families; the poor man's love is intensely concentrated on his wife and children. Wife and children do not always smile and prattle. Want makes them sad and serious. Cold and hunger and nakedness give them haggard looks, and then the poor man's heart bleeds at night as he tosses on his restless pillow. They are often delicate and sometimes sick. The parent must go out to toil to provide for them, nevertheless. He cannot watch over their sick beds like the rich. Apprehension does not sweeten and lighten his labors. Nor does loss of rest in watching and nursing a sick wife or child better fit him to earn his wages the next day. The poor have not the cares of wealth, but the greater cares of being without it. They have no houses, know not when they may be turned out of rented ones, or when, or on what terms they may rent another. This must be looked to and provided for. The head of the family gets sick sometimes, too. Wages cease. Does it soothe fever and assuage pain to look at a destitute family, or to reflect on the greater destitution that awaits them, if he, the parent, should die? Is he in health and getting good wages—the competition of fellow-laborers may any day reduce his wages or turn him out of employment. The poor free man has all the cares of the rich, and a thousand more besides. When the labors of the day are ended, domestic anxieties and cares begin. The usual, the ordinary, the normal condition of the whole laboring class, is that of physical suffering, cankering, corroding care, and mental apprehension and pain. The poor houses and poor rates prove this. The ragged beggar

children in the streets, and their suffering parents
pining in cellars and garrets, attest it. Destitute
France, poor Scotland, and starving Ireland pro-
claim it. The concurrent testimony of all history
and of all statistics, for three centuries, leave no
room for cavil or for doubt. Why, in this age of
progress, are the great majority of mankind, in
free countries, doomed to live in penitential pains
and purgatorial agony? They, the artificers of
every luxury, of every comfort, and every necessary of life, see the idle enjoying the fruits of their
toil. Is there a just God in Heaven, and does he
see, approve and ordain all this? Has it ever
been thus? If so, God delights in human agony,
and created man to punish him. All other animals enjoy life, and did God make man after his
own image, that life should be a pain and a tor-
ture to him? Bad as the laboring man's condition is now, those who live in free society tell us
it was far worse formerly. He used to be a slave,
and they say slavery is a far worse condition to
the laborer than liberty. Well, for the argument,
we grant it. His condition was worse throughout
all past times in slavery, than now with liberty.
Is it consistent with the harmony of nature, or
the wisdom and mercy of God, that such a being
should be placed in this world, and placed, too,
at the head of it? It is rank Diabolism to admit
such a conclusion. None but Lucifer would have
made such a world.

God made no such world! He instituted slavery from the first, as he instituted marriage and parental authority. Profane, presumptuous, ignorant man, in attempting to improve, has marred and defaced the work of his Creator. Wife and children, although not free, are relieved from care and anxiety, supported and protected, and their situation is as happy and desirable as that of the husband and parent. In this we see the doings of a wise and just God. The slave, too, when the night comes, may lie down in peace. He has a master to watch over and take care of him. If he be sick, that master will provide for him. If his family be sick, his master and mistress sympathise with his affliction, and procure medical aid for the sick. And when he comes to die, he feels that his family will be provided for. He does all the labor of life; his master bears all its corroding cares and anxieties. Here, again, we see harmonious relations, consistent with the wisdom and mercy of God. We see an equal and even-handed justice meted out to all alike, and we see life itself no longer a terrestrial purgatory; but a season of joy and sorrow to the rich and the poor.

Man is naturally associative, because isolated and alone he is helpless. The object of all associations, from States to Temperance societies, is mutual insurance. Man does not feel the advan-

tage of State insurance, until he is driven to the
poor house. House insurance companies and life
insurance companies often fail; and when successful, only insure against a class of misfortunes.
The insurance of Trade Unions, Odd Fellows,
and Temperance societies, is wholly inadequate.
Slavery insurance never fails, and covers all losses
and all misfortunes. Domestic slavery is nature's
mutual insurance society; art in vain attempts to
imitate it, or to supply its place.

CHAPTER XVII.

LIBERTY AND FREE TRADE.

These are convertible terms; two names for the same thing. Statesmen, orators, and philosophers, the tories of England, and the whigs of America, have been laboring incessantly for more than half a century to refute the doctrine of free trade. They all and each failed to produce a single plausible argument in reply. Not one of their books or speeches survived a month. Not one ever was, or ever will be, quoted or relied on as authority to disprove the principles of political economy. The reason is obvious enough; they were all confused by words, or afraid to make the proper issue. They first admitted liberty to be a good, and then attempted, but attempted in vain, to argue that free trade was an evil. The socialists stumbled on the true issue, but do not seem yet fully aware of the nature of their discovery. Liberty was the evil, liberty the disease under which society was suffering. It must be restricted, competition be arrested, the strong be restrained from, instead of encouraged to oppress the weak—in order to restore society to a healthy state. To them we are indebted for our argument against free trade. We have

H

extended it and explained its application. *They* demonstrated that social free trade was an evil, because it incited the rich and strong to oppress the weak, poor and ignorant. *We* saw that the disparities of mental strength were greater between races and nations than between individuals in the same society. History spoke less equivocally as to the ruinous effects of international free trade, than as to those of social free trade.

Events are occurring every day, especially at the North, that show that religious liberty must be restricted as well as other liberty.

Chinese idolaters are coming in swarms too, to California. If they are to be permitted to practise their diabolical rights, the negroes should be allowed to revert to the time-honored customs of their ancestors, and immolate human victims to their devil deity. Mormonism is still a worse religious evil, which we have to deal with.

Liberty is an evil which government is intended to correct. This is the sole object of government. Taking these premises, it is easy enough to refute free trade. Admit liberty to be a good, and you leave no room to argue that free trade is an evil,—because liberty is free trade.

With thinking men, the question can never arise, who ought to be free? Because no one ought to be free. All government is slavery. The proper subject of investigation for philosophers and philanthropists is, "Is the existin mode of ov-.

ernment adapted to the wants of its subjects?"
No one will contend that negroes, for instance,
should roam at large in puris naturalibus, with the
apes and tigers of Africa, and "worry and devour each other." Nor are they fitted for an
Athenian democracy. What form of government
short of domestic slavery will suit their wants
and capacities? That is the true issue, and we
direct the attention of abolitionists to it. They
are now striking wild, and often hit the Bible,
and marriage tie, and the right of property, and
the duties of children to their parents and guardians, harder blows, than they do negro slavery.
They are mere anarchists and infidels. If they
would take our advice, they would appear more
respectable, do less harm, and might suggest some
good. For domestic slavery like all human institutions, has its imperfections—will always have
them. Yet it is our duty to correct such as can
be corrected, and we would do so, if the abolitionists would let us alone, or advise with us as
friends, neighbors and gentlemen.

CHAPTER XVIII.

HEAD-WORK AND HAND-WORK.

Parents often warn their children, that they must live by hand-work or head-work. That the latter is far preferable, because the work is lighter, pays much better, and is generally in far higher esteem with the world. Virtue, intelligence and good education are necessary to success in the latter. No man cares much what the character of his ditcher or ploughman is, but his merchant, his lawyer, his mechanics, and his physician must be men of good sense and good morals. Thus do parents hold out incentives to virtuous exertion. Governors and rulers should do the same. States must live by hand-work or head-work. The production of books on the various arts and sciences, and on other subjects, the manufacture of fine silks, woolens, calicoes, shawls, the making of exquisite porcelain, the building of ships, and steamboats, the construction of machinery, and a thousand other pursuits that we could enumerate, require intelligence and attainments of the highest order, and good character besides, else no one would buy what would probably be a cheat or a counterfeit. A nation chiefly engaged in such pursuits, follows head-work, works within doors, labors lightly, and makes five times as much as one engaged in the coarsest occupations of mere hand-work. There cannot be a surplus population with such a people, because they have the world for a market to buy and sell in, and the more dense and numerous the population, the better opportunities are afforded for the association and division of labor, which increase its productiveness and lighten its burdens.

The very reverse of all this has been, till lately, the policy and practice of the South, inculcated and encouraged by her so called philosophers and statesmen. She has pursued the very lowest and coarsest hand-work,—work which required neither character nor intelligence, and which shut out the light of education, by rendering education unnecessary, or when necessary, making it impracticable from the sparseness of population. She has worked hard and been badly paid. On an average, the products of four hours of her hand work are exchanged for the results of one hour of such light work as we first described.

Peoples and individuals must live by hand-work, or head-work, and those who live by head-work are always, *in fact*, the masters of those who live by hand-work. They take the products of their labor without paying an equivalent in equal labor. The hand-work men and nations are slaves in fact, because they do not get paid for more than one-fourth of their labor. The South has, heretofore, worked three hours for Europe and the North, and one for herself. It is one of the beautiful results of free trade.

CHAPTER XIX.

An essay on the subject of slavery would be very imperfect, if it passed over without noticing these instruments. The abstract principles which they enunciate, we candidly admit, are wholly at war with slavery; we shall attempt to show that they are equally at war with all government, all subordination, all order. Men's minds were heated and blinded when they were written, as well by patriotic zeal, as by a false philosophy, which, beginning with Locke, in a refined materialism, had ripened on the Continent into open infidelity. In England, the doctrine of prescriptive government, of the divine right of kings, had met with signal overthrow, and in France there was faith in nothing, speculation about everything. The human mind became extremely presumptuous, and undertook to form governments on exact philosophical principles, just as men make clocks, watches or mills. They confounded the moral with the physical world, and this was not strange, because they had begun to doubt whether there was any other than a physical world. Society seemed to them a thing whose movement and action could be controlled with as much certainty as the motion of a spinning wheel, provided it was organized on proper principles. It would have been less presumptuous in them to have attempted to have made a tree, for a tree is not half so complex as a society of human beings, each of whom is fearfully and wonderfully compounded of soul and body, and whose aggregate, society, is still more complex and difficult of comprehension than its individual members. Trees grow and man may lop, trim, train and cultivate them, and thus hasten their growth, and improve their size, beauty and fruitfulness. Laws, institutions, societies, and governments grow, and men may aid their growth, improve their strength and beauty, and lop off their deformities and excrescences, by punishing crime and rewarding virtue. When society has worked long enough, under the hand of God and nature, man observing its operations, may discover its laws and constitution. The common law of England and the constitution of England, were discoveries of this kind. Fortunately for us, we adopted, with little change, that common law and that constitution. Our institutions and our ancestry were English. Those institutions were the growth and accretions of many ages, not the work of legislating philosophers.

The abstractions contained in the various instruments on which we professed, but professed falsely, to found our governments, did no harm, because, until abolition arose, they remained a dead letter. Now, and not till now, these abstractions have become matters of serious practical importance, and we propose to give some of them a candid, but fearless examination. We find these words in the preamble and Declaration of Independence,

"We hold these truths to be self-evident, that all men are created equal; that they are endowed by their Creator with certain inalienable rights, that among them, are life, liberty, and the pursuit of happiness; that to secure these rights governments are instituted among men, deriving their just powers from the consent of the governed; that whenever any form of government becomes destructive of these ends it is the right of the people to alter or abolish it, and to institute a new government, laying its foundations on such principles, and organizing its powers in such form, as to them shall seem most likely to effect their safety and happiness."

It is, we believe, conceded on all hands, that men are not born physically, morally or intellectually equal,—some are males, some females, some from birth, large, strong and healthy, others weak, small and sickly—some are naturally amiable, others prone to all kinds of wickednesses—some brave, others timid.   Their natural inequalities beget inequalities of rights.   The weak in mind or body require guidance, support and protection; they must obey and work for those who protect and guide them—they have a natural right to guardians, committees, teachers or masters.   Nature has made them slaves; all that law and government can do, is to regulate, modify and mitigate their slavery.   In the absence of legally instituted slavery, their condition would be worse under that natural slavery of the weak to the strong, the foolish to the wise and cunning.   The wise and virtuous, the brave, the strong in mind and body, are by nature born to command and protect, and law but follows nature in making them rulers, legislators, judges, captains, husbands, guardians, committees and masters.   The naturally depraved class, those born prone to crime, are our brethren too; they are entitled to education, to religious instruction, to all the means and appliances proper to correct their evil propensities, and all their failings; they have a right to be sent to the penitentiary,—for there, if they do not reform, they cannot at least disturb society.   Our feelings, and our consciences teach us, that nothing but necessity can justify taking human life.   ·

We are but stringing together truisms, which every body knows as well as ourselves, and yet

if men are created unequal in all these respects,
what truth or what meaning is there in the passage under consideration? Men are not created
or born equal, and circumstances, and education,
and association, tend to increase and aggravate
inequalities among them, from generation to generation. Generally, the rich associate and intermarry with each other, the poor do the same;
the ignorant rarely associate with or intermarry
with the learned, and all society shuns contact
with the criminal, even to the third and fourth
generations.

Men are not " born entitled to equal rights!"
It would be far nearer the truth to say, "that
some were born with saddles on their backs, and
others booted and spurred to ride them,"—and
the riding does them good. They need the reins,
the bit and the spur. No two men by nature are
exactly equal or exactly alike. No institutions
can prevent the few from acquiring rule and as-
cendency over the many. Liberty and free competition invite and encourage the attempt of the
strong to master the weak; and insure their success.

" Life and liberty" are not "inalienable;" they
have been sold in all countries, and in all ages,
and must be sold so long as human nature lasts.
It is an inexpedient and unwise, and often unmerciful restraint, on a man's liberty of action, to

deny him the right to sell himself when starving, and again to buy himself when fortune smiles. Most countries of antiquity, and some, like China at the present day, allowed such sale and purchase. The great object of government is to restrict, control and punish man "in the pursuit of happiness." All crimes are committed in its pursuit. Under the free or competitive system, most men's happiness consists in destroying the happiness of other people. This, then, is no inalienable right.

The author of the Declaration may have, and probably did mean, that all men were created with an equal title to property. Carry out such a doctrine, and it would subvert every government on earth.

In practice, in all ages, and in all countries, men had sold their liberty either for short periods, for life, or hereditarily; that is, both their own liberty and that of their children after them. The laws of all countries have, in various forms and degrees, in all times recognised and regulated this right to *alien* or sell liberty. The soldiers and sailors of the revolution had aliened both liberty and life, the wives in all America had aliened their liberty, so had the apprentices and wards at the very moment this verbose, new-born, false and unmeaning preamble was written.

Mr. Jefferson was an enthusiastic speculative philosopher; Franklin was wise, cunning and judicious; he made no objection to the Declaration, as prepared by Mr. Jefferson, because, probably, he saw it would suit the occasion and supposed it would be harmless for the future. But even Franklin was too much of a physical philosopher, too utilitarian and material in his doctrines, to be relied on in matters of morals or government. We may fairly conclude, that liberty is alienable, that there is a natural right to alien it, first, because the laws and institutions of all countries have recognized and regulated its alienation; and secondly, because we cannot conceive of a civilized society, in which there were no wives, no wards, no apprentices, no sailors and no soldiers; and none of these could there be in a country that practically carried out the doctrine, that liberty is inalienable.

The soldier who meets death at the cannon's mouth, does so because he has aliened both life and liberty. Nay, more, he has aliened the pursuit of happiness, else he might desert on the eve of battle, and pursue happiness in some more promising quarter than the cannon's mouth. If the pursuit of happiness be inalienable, men should not be punished for crime, for all crimes are notoriously committed in the pursuit of happiness. If these abstractions have some hidden and cabalistic meaning, which none but the initiated can comprehend, then the Declaration should have been accompanied with a translation, and a commentary to fit it for common use,—as it stands, it deserves the tumid yet appropriate epithets which Major Lee somewhere applies to the writings of Mr. Jefferson, it is, "exhuberantly false, and arborescently fallacious."

Nothing can be found in all history more unphilosophical, more presumptuous, more characteristic of the infidel philosophy of the 18th century, than the language that follows that of which we have been treating. How any observant man, however unread, should have come to the conclusion, that society and government were such plastic, man-created things, that starting on certain general principles, he might frame them successfully as he pleased, we are at a loss to conceive. But infidelity is blind and foolish, and infidelity then prevailed. Lay your foundations of government on what principles you please, organize its powers in what form you choose, and you cannot foresee the results. You can only tell what laws, institutions and governments will effect, when you apply them to the same race or nation under the same circumstances in which they have already been tried. But philosophy then was in the chrysalis state. She has since deluged the world with blood, crime and pauperism. She has had full sway, and has inflicted much misery, and done no good. The world is beginning to be satisfied, that it is much safer and better, to look to the past, to trust to experience, to follow nature, than to be guided by the ignis fatuus of *a priori* speculations of closet philosophers. If all men had been created equal, all would have been competitors, rivals, and enemies. Subordination, difference of caste and classes, difference of sex, age and slavery beget peace and good will.

We were only justified in declaring our independence, because we were sufficiently wise, numerous and strong to govern ourselves, and too distant and distinct from England to be well governed by her.

Moses and Confucius, Solon, Lycurgus and English Alfred, were Reformers, Revisors of the Code. They, too, were philosophers, but too profound to mistake the province of philosophy and attempt to usurp that of nature. They did not frame government on abstract principles, they indulged in no "*a priori*" reasoning; but simply lopped off what was bad, and retained, modified and simplified what was good in existing institutions—

"And that's as high,
As metaphysic wit can fly."

The first clause of the Bill of Rights of Virginia, contains language of like import with that which we have been criticising. The fourth clause

is in the following words :—"That no man or set of
men are entitled to exclusive or separate privileges
from the rest of the community, but in consideration of public services : which not being discendi-
ble, neither ought the offices of magistrate, legis-
lator or judge, to be hereditary." This is very
bad English and is so obscurely expressed, that
we can only guess at the meaning intended to be
conveyed. We suppose, that "exclusive or separate emoluments and privileges," was intended to
apply to such harmless baubles as titles of nobility and coats of arms, and to petty ill-paid officers, and that the author never dreamed that hereditary property, however large, was a "separate
emolument or privilege."

The author saw no objection to the right se-
cured by law to hold five hundred subjects or
negro slaves, and ten thousand acres of land, to
the exclusion of everybody else, and to trans-
mit them to one's children and grand-children,
although an exclusive hereditary privilege far
transcending any held by the nobility of Europe,—for the nobility of Russia do not hold
such despotic sway over their serfs, as we do
over our negroes, and are themselves mere slaves
to the Emperor, whilst our slaveholders have
scarcely any authority above them. We have
no doubt the author, like our modern farmers, considered this "a mere circumstance,"

and would have told you that a man has a *natural right* to his lands and negroes, a natural right to what belonged to his father.

Property is not a natural and divine, but conventional right; it is the mere creature of society and law. In this all lawyers and publicists agree. In this country, the history of property is of such recent date, that the simplest and most ignorant man must know, that it commenced in wrong, injustice and violence a few generations ago, and derives its only title now from the will of society through the sanction of law. Society has no right, because it is not expedient, to resume any one man's property because he abuses its possession, and does not so employ it as to redound to public advantage,—but if all private property, or if private property generally were so used as to injure, instead of promote public good, then society might and ought to destroy the whole institution.

From these premises, it follows that government, in taxing private property, should only be limited by the public good. If the tax be so heavy as to deter the owner from improving the property, then, in general, will the whole public be injured.

False notions of the right of property, and of the duties and liabilities of property holders, destroy all public spirit and patriotism, cripple and injure, and prevent the growth and development of the South. We feel it our duty to deflect a little from our subject to expose these errors.

Now, a natural right is a "divine right," and if we Southern farmers have a divine right to our little realms and subjects, is it not hard to dispute the like right in sovereigns, on a larger scale. The world discovered that the power of kings was a trust power conferred on them for the good of the people, and to be exercised solely for that purpose—or else forfeited. Are we guilty of treason in suggesting that farmers have no better titles than kings, and that the LAW vests them with separate property in lands and negroes, under the belief and expectation that such separate property will redound more to public advantage than if all property were in common? We have an aristocracy with more of privilege, and less of public spirit, than any that we meet with in history. Less of public spirit, because they cherish that free trade philosophy which inculcates selfishness as a moral and political duty, which teaches that the public good is best promoted when nobody attends to public affairs, but each one is intent on his own private ends. Naturally, Southerners, like all slaveholders, are liberal and public spirited. It is their philosophy that has taken away their patriotism. According to the sense in which the term "public services" is used, meaning, no doubt, official services, in the Bill of Rights, no farmer could hold his lands and negroes a day, for they have not rendered public services as a consideration for their great, "exclusive and separate emolument and privilege."

Institutions are what men can see, feel, venerate and understand. The institutions of Moses and of Alfred remain to this day, those of Numa and Lycurgus had a long and flourishing life. These sages laid down no abstract propositions, founded their institutions on no general principles, had no written *constitutions*. They were wise from experience, adopted what history and experience had tested, and never trusted to *a priori* speculations, like a More, a Locke, a Jefferson, or an Abbe Sieyes. Constitutions should never be written till several centuries after governments have been instituted, for it requires that length of time to ascertain how institutions will operate. No matter how you define and limit, in words, the powers and duties of each department of government, they will each be sure to exercise as much power as possible, and to encroach to the utmost of their ability on the powers of other departments. When the Commons were invoked to Parliament, the king had no idea they would usurp the taxing powers; but having successfully done so, it became part of the English constitution, that the people alone could tax themselves. It was never intended that ninety-nine guilty should escape, sooner than one innocent man be punished; yet, finding that the result of the English judicial system, the judges and lawyers made a merit of necessity, and adopted it as a maxim of the common law. So, in a hundred instances we could show, that in England a constitution means the modus operandi of institutions, not prescribed, but ascertained from experience. In this country we shall soon have two constitutions, that *a priori* thing which nobody regards, and that practical constitution deduced from observation of the workings of our institutions.— Whigs disregard our written constitution, when banks, tariffs or internal improvements are in question; Democrats respect it not when there is a chance to get more territory; and Young America, the dominant party of the day, will jump through its paper obstructions with as much dexterity as harlequin does through the hoop. State governments, and senators, and representatives, and militia, and cities, and churches, and colleges, and universities, and landed property, are institutions. Things of flesh and blood, that know their rights, "and knowing dare maintain them." We should cherish them. They will give permanence to government, and security to State Rights. But the abstract doctrines of nullification and secession, the general principles laid down in the Declaration of Independence, the Bill of Rights, and Constitution of the United States, afford no protection of rights, no valid limitations of power, no security to State Rights. The power to construe them, is the power to nullify them. Mere paper guarantees, like the constitutions of Abbe Sieyes, are as worthless as the paper on which they are written.

Our institutions, founded on such generalities and abstractions as those of which we are treating, are like a splendid edifice built upon kegs of gunpowder. The abolitionists are trying to apply the match to the explosive materials under our Parliament House; we are endeavoring to anticipate them by drenching those materials with ridicule. No body deems them worth the trouble of argument, or the labor of removal. They will soon become incombustible and innocuous.

Property is too old and well-tried an institution, too much interwoven with the feelings, interests, prejudices and affections of man, to be shaken by the speculations of philosophers. It is only its mal-administration that can endanger it. So far from wishing to shake or undermine property, we would, for the public good, give it more permanence. We do not like the Western Homestead provision of forty acres, because that entails on families poverty and ignorance, and tends to depress civilization. We do not like the large entails of England, because they beget an idle, useless and vicious aristocracy. But lands do not breed as men do, and we can see no good public reason for cutting up small farms, at the end of each generation, and thus preventing good and permanent improvements, and incurring the oft-repeated labor of making new enclosures, and new but slight buildings. For public good, and property ought to be administered for public good, it would be better to have some law of primogeniture where the lands were of a convenient size to keep together. A law entailing farms of such amount as would educate families well, without putting them above the necessity of industry and exertion, would add much to national wealth, in encouraging good and permanent improvements, and would improve national character and intelligence, by securing a class of well educated men, attached to the soil and the country. We need not fear the mad dog-cry of aristocracy; a man with an entailed estate of five hundred acres, and a coat of arms to boot, would not be a very dangerous character. Whilst men with twenty thousand acres of illy cultivated lands and five hundred idle negroes, or bankers wielding five millions, all of which they may entail or settle in their families for generations to come, are to all intents and purposes, as good aristocrats as any German Princes. We have the *things*, exclusive hereditary privileges and aristocracy, amongst us, in their utmost intensity; let us not be frightened at the *names;* but so mould our institutions, regardless of prejudices, technicalities, names, or titles, as will best promote, "the greatest good of the greatest number."

Too much insecurity of property invites to extravagance and speculation, and prevents refinement and continued progress. Property should remain several generations in a family to beget learning, skill, and high moral qualifications.

Lands divided minutely, depress all pursuits; for small farms want only coarse and cheap articles, quack doctors, illiterate parsons, and ignorant attorneys. When farms are too large, they occasion a sparse population, absenteeism of the rich, and a sort of colonial or plantation life. Either extreme is equally to be avoided, and, therefore, the State should determine the amount of land subject to the laws of primogeniture and entail. Such laws might be enacted without any shock to existing titles, and would vastly enhance the value of our lands. People who are tired, (and half the world is,) of the too frequent ups and downs of American life, would rush to Virginia to invest their money. If other States did not follow our example, Virginia would, in five years, be the first State in wealth and intelligence in the Union. If such arrangement be best for all society, then it is the most democratic arrangement, for it is the essence of democracy to consult the good of the whole. Landed *property* thus held, would become an *institution* attaching its owners to our government. Patriotism and love of country, virtues now unknown at the South, would prevail, and give permanence and security to society.

No great advantages accrue to society, either in wealth, morals, or intelligence, by the frequent change of property from hand to hand, and from family to family. Lands would become useless, if minutely divided between all the members of the community. The law now devolves lands in case of intestacy on all a man's children. The laws of most countries have devolved them on the male children, or on one child. None have a natural right to them. If it be expedient that they should descend to one child, and be continued in the family, there is nothing in natural justice or equity to oppose the arrangement. Five hundred acres of land and thirty negroes, would suffice to educate all the younger members of the family, and make useful citizens of them. Primogeniture and entails have had this good effect in England. The younger sons have filled the professions, the church, the army, and the navy, with able, ambitious men. It has furnished London and Liverpool with the best merchants in the world, and made trade one of the most honorable professions.

It is pleasing to see the poor acquiring lands, but the pleasure is more than balanced, with all save the malicious, by seeing the rich stripped of them. Those accustomed to poverty, suffer little from it. Those who have been rich, are miserable when they become poor.

CHAPTER XX.

THE MARRIAGE RELATION.

The Roman dwelling was a holy and sacred place; a temple of the gods, over which Manes, and Lares, and Penates watched and hovered. Each hearthstone was an altar on which daily sacrifice was offered. The family was hedged all round with divinities, with departed ancestry purified and apotheosised, who with kindly interest guarded and guided the household. Roman elevation of sentiment and of character is easily accounted for, when we reflect that they felt themselves ever in the presence of deities. That pure religious sentiment was associated with these deities, a single passage from Virgil will prove. Æneas, on that night that Troy was sacked, forced at length to fly with his family, does not forget in his haste and confusion, the family gods.

> Tu, genitor, cape sacra manu, patriosque Penates.
> Me, bello è tanto digressum, et cæde recenti
> Attrectare nefas. donec me flumine vivo
> Abluero.

The Catholic Church did much to preserve the sanctity and purity of the family circle, by making

marriage a religious sacrament; the Episcopal
Church something in making it a holy ordinance;
and in its ritual, which reminded the parties of
the solemn and sacred engagements into which
they were about to enter. But as liberty, equality
and fraternity advanced, it was reduced, at the
free North, to a mere civil contract, entered into
with no more thought, ceremony or solemnity than
the bargain for a horse. We shall not sully our
sheet with descriptions of the marriage relation
as it often presents itself now, even in good society
in free Europe and in free America. Shakers,
and Oneida Perfectionists and Mormons, are the
legitimate fruits of modern progress. Surely
women ought to be free as well as negroes. In
Utah, (the highest and latest result of liberty,
equality, and fraternity,) the family dwelling,
which in heathen Rome was a temple of the
Gods, has been converted into a den of prosti-
tutes. What a rise, from pious and pagan
Æneas, to Brigham Young the Yankee Christian
of the latest cut and newest fashion!

CHAPTER XXI.

THE MORALS OF FREE SOCIETY.

Let heav'n kiss earth! Now let not nature's hand
Keep the wild flood confin'd! let order die!
And let this world no longer be a stage,
To feed contention in a lingering act;
But let one spirit of the first-born Cain
Reign in all bosoms, that each heart being set
On bloody courses, the rude scene may end
And darkness be the burier of the dead!

SECOND PART OF KING HENRY IV.

"Liberty, Equality and Fraternity," is the motto and watchword of Frenchmen when they turn out to murder each other wholesale. They are an epigramatic people, and have a happy way of condensing into a phrase or maxim, a whole code of philosophy. The same idea had been floating in men's minds ever since the Reformation

"What oft was thought, but ne'er so well expressed."

It had borne, too, everywhere the same fruits. The seventy years' wars in Germany are further off in time and distance than the French Revolution, but were quite as prolific of murder, rape and rapine, as those amiable events themselves. They were the first exhibitions on a large scale, of the new philosophy of Liberty, Equality and

Fraternity. The revocation of the edict of Nantes, and the Vespers of St. Bartholemew, were small events compared to the days of the Guillotine; but nevertheless, they were highly respectable and intense expressions of that fraternity which nascent liberty was begetting. The Gunpowder plot, too, but for an unlucky *contre temps,* would have resulted in a very strong expression of the affectionate brotherly interest which men feel for one another's well being, both in this world and the world to come. Shortly thereafter, when liberty openly reared her standard, and Cromwell burnt houses, and Sir Thomas Lunsford ate babies, men began to believe that the world was really blessed with the millenial advent of Liberty, Equality and Fraternity. Charles and Jeffries put a stop to it for a while: yet towards the later part of his reign, Charles wisely resolved to give a holyday, and indulge his people with a bloody carnival. The little Titus Oates affair that followed, showed that men's affections for each other had not at all abated, and were ready to exhibit themselves in the most passionate manner, whenever the restraints of government were removed.

Our Pilgrim fathers being denied the opportunity of practicing to its full extent the divine precept—" Love thy neighbor as thyself "—removed to America, and here proved to the world that they had not degenerated since the unctuous days of Knox and of Cromwell. Many tokens of their zeal and affection were soon seen pendant from the elms of New England; and with a delicate discrimination, that affection selected the ugliest and oldest of the weaker sex, on whom to lavish its embraces.

Has the world "supped full with horrors," or a mere caprice of fashion brought about new modes of manifesting attachment? Frenchmen kiss and hug, Americans shake hands, and Englishmen scowl and bow; yet they all mean the same thing—'tis fashion rules the hour. So it may be that cheating and starving our fellow beings is now the rage, instead of shooting and burning them. Those three hundred thousand starved in Ireland, show clearly enough that Liberty, Equality and Fraternity have lost none of their energy, however much they may have quieted their manners. "*Nil admirari*" is the perfection of good breeding in England, and a real gentleman would sooner cheat in a horse trade than express sympathy for the millions who are pining with hunger and nakedness in the fields and factories and mines of old England.

We should do gross injustice to our own fellow countrymen if we failed to notice a little "Love Feast" that occurred a few days ago in St. Louis. The killed and wounded would have been a trifle in Paris, but did pretty well for new beginners. It was a genteel and select affair, for not a negro was permitted to fraternise. Generally, these affairs are decidedly vulgar in America, in consequence of the great love of the Northern folk for the negroes. In Philadelphia and Cincinnati, some little Love Feasts have been enacted for the benefit of our black brethren, who, when the feasts were over, found themselves stript of clothes and trowsers—sans eyes, sans ears, sans teeth, sans every thing. These, and other striking evidences of brotherly interest, such as brick-bats and glass bottles, leave Sambo no room to doubt that he is a peculiar favorite,—yet Sambo, who is a quiet body, is getting heartily tired of such rough romping and hard love-licks.

Liberty, Equality and Fraternity, culminated when the Goddess of Reason usurped the seat and the sceptre of Deity, and sent forth her high priests, Danton, Marat, St. Just and Robespierre, "to deal damnation round the land!" The demonstration was then complete. Man without government, without order, without subordination, without religion, without slavery in its every form, from the prison house, the straight jacket, the army, the navy, serfdom, up to the slavery of mere subjection to law, without all those restraints which his peculiar wants and capacities required, was the cruellest and wildest beast of the field.

It proved that a state of nature was not a state of liberty, for a state of liberty is a state of exterminating warfare. It proved that neither religion nor morality could exist without enough of government to enforce the performance of duty on each member of society.

We have attempted, elsewhere, to show, that there cannot be enough of such government without domestic slavery, because, in its absence, men are placed in competitive and antagonistic positions toward each other. This separation of interest and antagonism begets continual rivalry, hatred, and intense discord and war, which political economy exasperates and increases, by encouraging exclusive devotion to men's self-interest. A celebrated Socialist properly calls it "the philosophy of self interest."

But political economy is the necessary result of Free Society—it is the only moral code which it can inculcate—and yet all its precepts are at war with morality. But for Christianity, Free Society would be a wilderness of crime; and Christianity has not fair play and a proper field of action, where government has failed to institute the peace-begetting and protective influence of domestic slavery. It is one of the necessary parts of government, without which men become enemies instead of brethren. There is no love between equals, and the divine precept, "Love thy neighbor as thyself," is thundered vainly in the ears of men straining for the same object.

The maxim, "every man for himself," embraces the whole moral code of Free Society; and Miss Bremer, and all the other philanthropists in the world, with their thousand schemes and institutions, will never be able to neutralise the immoral and death dealing tendency of that maxim, and of the antagonism and social war that it generates.

CHAPTER XXII.

SMALL NATIONALITIES.

Almost the only secret of high civilization and national greatness consists in narrow and confined territorial limits. Beget the necessity for the exercise of all the functions of government, all the mechanic and artistic arts, for the cultivation of all the sciences, and for the pursuit of all the avocations of civilized life by a small population, and intense enlightenment and universal education are the immediate result. History, ancient and modern, teaches but one lesson on this subject. Little Phœnicia and little Carthage, the hundred little states of Greece, and Rome, whilst her dominion was confined to Italy, were truly great. When Alexander had conquered Egypt and Persia, and died for want of other worlds to conquer, Greece fell to rise no more, and in her fall involved the conquered nations in one common ruin. Rome conquered the world, and forthwith Cimmerian darkness began to cover her empire. England, under the Plantagenets, ere Scotland or Ireland were annexed, crowned her King in Paris. Now, whilst the beat of her drum circles the globe, she trembles at the threat of French invasion.

Little Prussia, little Venice, little Holland, and little Portugal, have each, in turn, controlled the destines of Europe. Even little Sweden, under Charles XII., whipped all the Russias till she taught Peter how to fight. Overgrown nations, like overgrown men, want energy, activity and intelligence.

We should learn from these instances in history to prize and guard State Rights. We should, as far as consistent with the Constitution, make each State independent of the rest of the world ; create a necessity for the exercise of all the arts, sciences, trades, professions and other pursuits that pertain to separate nationality ; and endeavor to counteract the centralizing tendency of modern improvements in locomotion and intercommunication, which naturally rob the extremities to enrich the centres of Power and of Trade. We live in critical times, for the tendency to centralization is stronger than ever before. Trade very easily effects now what conquest did formerly. Let the States of the South look to this matter. Are they willing to remain mere colonies and plantations for the centres of trade, or will they preserve their separate nationality ?

CHAPTER XXIII.

THE HIGHER LAW.

In framing and revising the institutions and government of a nation, and in enacting its laws, sensible and prudent statesmen study carefully the will of God and designs of Providence, as revealed in Holy Writ, or as gathered from history and experience. "Truth is mighty, and will prevail," and laws in contravention of the great truths deducible from these sources, will become nugatory and inefficient. Yet whilst the law is on the statute book, every citizen is bound to respect and obey it, or else take the consequences of trespass, felony or treason. He may discuss the question, "Does the law coincide with the 'Higher Law'?" but he may not act on his conclusions if they be against the law.

Does slavery violate the Higher Law? Certainly not, if that Higher Law is to be found only in the Bible. Certainly not, if you throw aside the Bible, and infer what is right, proper, and natural, from the course of nature, the lessons of history, or the voice of experience. But consult the same sources for your Higher Law, and as certainly is free society a violation of the laws of Nature and the revealed will of God.

CHAPTER XXIV.

INFIDELITY AND ABOLITIONISM.

Every one who reads the newspapers must have observed that open-mouthed infidelity is never seen or heard in this country except in abolition meetings and conventions, and in women's rights conventicles. On such occasions some woman unsexes herself, and with Gorgon head and Harpy tongue pours out false and foul execrations against slavery and the Bible, aided by men with sharper tongues and duller courage than the women themselves. To this there is a single exception. One pulpit in Boston is on the Sabbath made a rostrum whence an abolitionist fulminates contention and discord, and stirs up to bloodshed and murder.

Liberty, infidelity, and abolition, are three words conveying but one idea. Infidels who dispute the authority of God will not respect or obey the government of man. Abolitionists, who make war upon slavery, instituted by God and approved by Holy Writ, are in a fair way to denounce the Bible that stands in the way of the attainment of their purpose. Marriage is too much like slavery not to be involved in its fate; and the obedience of wives which the Bible inculcates, furnishes a new theme for infidelity in petticoats or in Bloomers to harp on. Slavery, marriage, religion, are the pillars of the social fabric. France felled them at a blow, and Paris and St. Domingo were crushed beneath the ruins of the edifice which they supported.

Frenchmen and Germans are generally infidels, agrarians and abolitionists. An Irish infidel, an Irish agrarian, or an Irish abolitionist, is scarcely to be found. No Irish woman ever disgraces her own sex, or affects the dress and manners of the opposite sex. The men of Erin are all brave, patriotic and religious; her women are

> " Chaste as the icicle
> That's curdled by the frost of purest snow,
> And hangs on Dian's temple."

This intimate connexion and dependence, of slavery, marriage and religion, we suggest as a subject for the investigation and reflection of the reader. If ever the abolitionists succeed in thoroughly imbuing the world with their doctrines and opinions, all religion, all government, all order, will be slowly but surely subverted and destroyed. Society can linger on for centuries without slavery; it cannot exist a day without religion. As an institution of government, religion is strictly within the scope of our work, and as such we treat of it.

For fear assaults upon us may weaken the force of our facts and arguments, we will take occasion more strictly to define our opinions as to government. We have ever, and still do belong to the Democratic party;—not, however, to the "let alone" and "largest liberty" wing of that party. We believe in the capacity of the people to govern, and would not deny them the opportunity to exercise that capacity. We think there is no danger from too much or too popular government, provided we avoid centralization, and distribute as much as possible to small localities powers of police and legislation. We would cherish and preserve all our *institutions* as they are, adding to them probably larger separate governmental powers to be vested in the people of each county. The cause of popular government is on the advance. The printing press, railroads, steamships and the telegraph afford opportunities for information, consultation and combination. But these agencies, which will make governments more popular, will at the same time render them more efficient, all-pervading, rigid and exact. Ancient Republicanism will supplant Laissez-faire Republicanism;—and ancient Republicanism we admire and prefer.

CHAPTER XXV.

Reformations always do good, revolutions always harm. All old institutions in time become incrusted with error and abuse, and frequent reforms are required to keep them in good working order, and to adapt them to the gradually changing circumstances of mankind. This is equally true of religious institutions as of political ones, for there is much in the machinery and external manifestations of the former, that is of mere human origin and contrivance,—and everything human is liable to imperfection and decay.

Total changes, which revolutions propose, are never wise or practicable, because most of the institutions of every country are adapted to the manners, morals and sentiments of the people. Indeed, the people have been moulded in character by those institutions, and they cannot be torn asunder and others substituted, for none others will fit. Hence reforms result in permanent change and improvement. Revolutions, after a great waste of blood and treasure, leave things to return soon to the " status quo ante bellum." English statesmen, fully alive to these great truths, have for centuries past anticipated and prevented revolutions, by granting timely reforms. Mr. Jefferson, when we separated from Great Britain, wished to effect a total revolution, " laying its foundations on such principles, and organizing its powers in such forms, as," &c. Fortunately for us, the practical men who framed our government saw the wisdom and necessity of adopting English institutions (to which we had been accustomed), with very slight modifications, to adapt them to our circumstances. Our separation from England was a great and salutary reform, not a revolution. Scotland is now attempting a reform less in degree, but the same in character—she is trying to get back her parliament and to establish a separate nationality. We have no doubt it would redound to the strength and the glory of Great Britain, if both Scotland and Ireland had separate parliaments.

CHAPTER XXVI.

THE SLAVE TRADE.

From several quarters propositions have of late been made for the revival of the African slave trade. The South has generally been opposed to this trade, the North favorable to it. Such is likely to be the case again; for the North would make much money by conducting the trade; the settled states of the South lose much by the depreciation of their negroes. The extreme inhumanity of this trade is enough to condemn it, but men's interests blind their eyes and steel their hearts against considerations of humanity. Besides, the argument will be most successfully employed in its behalf, that it will but take the place of another kind of slave trade, that is still more inhuman. The importation of apprentices or temporary slaves is now actively conducted by England from Africa and various parts of Asia. These apprentices, if not worked to death before their terms of service expire, are left to starve afterwards, and new ones imported in their place. They are treated with less humanity than slaves, because the master has little interest in their lives. Vastly larger numbers must be imported to supply the demand for labor, because their children are not slaves, and they themselves but for a time. After liberation they will become a nuisance to the country that imports them.

The fact that, despite of the enormous annual importation of slaves to Cuba, the number of whites is greater than that of blacks in that island, proves clearly enough that where it is cheaper to buy African slaves than to rear them, men will work these poor natives to death, regardless of humanity. Besides, the natural antipathy between the savage and the civilized man, not only prevents the influence of domestic affection on the heart of the master, but indurates his feelings and degrades his morals. Our slaves are treated far better than they were forty years ago, because they have improved in mind and morals, approached nearer to the master's state of civilization, and thus elicited more of his interest and attachment. Slavery with us is becoming milder every day; were the slave trade revived, it would resume its pristine cruelty. The slaves we now hold would become less valuable, and we should take less care of them. In justice to them let us protest against the renewal of this infamous traffic. Slavery originating from the conquest of a country is beneficent even in its origin, for it preserves the slaves or serfs who are parcelled out to the conquering chiefs from the waste, pillage, cruelty and oppression of the common soldiers of the conquering army,—but slavery brought about by hunting and catching Africans like beasts, and then exposing them to the horrors of the middle passage, is quite a different thing.

We think it would be both wise and humane to subject the free negroes in America to some modification of slavery. Competition with the whites is killing them out. They are neither so moral, so happy, nor half so well provided as the slaves. Let them select their masters, and this would be another instance of slavery originating without violence or cruelty—another instance in which slavery would redress much greater evils than it occasioned.

CHAPTER XXVII.

WOMAN'S RIGHTS.

Slender.—I came yonder at Eton to marry mistress Anne Page, and she's a great lubberly boy. If it had not been i' the church, I would have swinged him, or he should have swinged me. If I did not think it had been Anne Page, would I might never stir, and 'tis a post-master's boy.—*Merry Wives of Windsor.*

Nothing in the signs of the times exhibits in stronger relief the fact, that free society is in a state "of dissolution and thaw," of demoralization and transition, than the stir about woman's rights. And yet it is time to work. Northern newspapers are filled with the sufferings of poor widowed needlewomen, and the murders of wives by their husbands. Woman *there* is in a false position. Be she white, or be she black, she is treated with kindness and humanity in the slave-holding South. In Asia, she ever has been and is now an idol, secluded from the vulgar gaze, and exempted from the hard and coarse labors of *man.* The Turks and the Chinese imprison. her, but worship her. Her veiled face and cramped feet, unfit her for work, condemn her to seclusion, but secure to her protection. She is a slave, but is idle, honored and caressed. The Romans girded up the toga, when about to engage in labor. If American women wish to participate in the hard labor of men, they are right to curtail the petticoat. Queens wear the longest trains, because they have least occasion to labor. The broom girls of Bavaria have to work hard for a living, and find it necessary to amputate the nether impediments. In France, woman draws the plough and the canal boat. She will be condemned to like labors in America, so soon as her dress, her education and coarse sentiments fit her for such labors. Let her exhibit strength and hardihood, and man, her master, will make her a beast of burden. So long as she is nervous, fickle, capricions, delicate, diffident and dependent, man will worship and adore her. Her weakness is her strength, and her true art is to cultivate and improve that weakness. Woman naturally shrinks from public gaze, and from the struggle and competition of life. Free society has thrown her into the arena of industrial war, robbed her of the softness of her own sex, without conferring on her the strength of ours. In truth, woman, like children, has but one right, and that is the right to protection. The right to protection involves the obligation to obey. A husband, a lord and master, whom she should love, honor and obey, nature designed for every woman,—for the number of males and females is the same. If she be

obedient, she is in little danger of mal-treatment;
if she stands upon her rights, is coarse and masculine, man loathes and despises her, and ends by
abusing her. Law, however well intended, can
do little in her behalf. True womanly art will
give her an empire and a sway far greater than
she deserves. The best women have been dis-
tasteful to men, and unpopular with their own sex,
simply for betraying, or seeming to betray, something masculine in their characters. Catherine
Parr, Miss Edgeworth, Mrs. Fry, Miss Martineau,
and Madame De Stael, are not loveable characters. On the other hand, men have adored the
worst women, merely for their feminine charms
and arts. Rhodope and Aspasia, Delilah, Cleo-
patra, Mary Stuart, Ninon D'Enclos, Maria Antoi-
nette, Herodias and Lola Montez, ruled men as
they pleased, by the exercise of all the charms,
and more than the wiles and weakness of their
sex. Mrs. Stowe, in the characters of Aunt
Phebe and Mrs. St. Clair, beautifully illustrates
and enforces this idea. Bad as Mrs. St. Clair is,
we feel that we might love her, but good Aunt
Phebe is a she-man, continually boring and el-
bowing us with her rectangular virtues. Yet Mrs.
Stowe would have women preach. If she sets
them to preaching to-day, we men will put them
to the plough to-morrow. Women would do well

to disguise strength of mind or body, if they possess it, if they would retain their empire.

The people of our Northern States, who hold that domestic slavery is unjust and iniquitous, are consistent in their attempts to modify or abolish the marriage relation. Marriages, in many places there, are contracted with as little formality as jumping over a broom, and are dissolved with equal facility by courts and legislatures. It is proposed by many to grant divorces at all times, when the parties mutually consent. The Socialists suggest that the relation should be abolished, private family establishments broken up, and women and children converted into joint stock. The ladies are promoting these movements by women's right's conventions. The prospects of these agitators are quite hopeful, because they have no conservative South to oppose them. It is their own affair, and we will not interfere with its regulation.

We shall deplore the day when marriage and Christianity are abolished anywhere, but will not interfere in the social and domestic matters of other people.

The men of the South take care of the women of the South, the men of slaveholding Asia guard and protect their women too. The generous sentiments of slaveholders are sufficient guarantee of the rights of woman, all the world over.

But there is something wrong in her condition in free society, and that condition is daily becoming worse.

Give us woman with all her frailties and infirmities, *varium et mutabalile semper.*

> "Like the uncertain glory of an April day
> Which now shows all the beauty of sun,
> And bye and bye a cloud takes all away!"

We like not that—

> ——"Beauty, forever unchangingly bright,
> Like the long sunny lapse of a summer's day light,
> Shining on, shining on, by no shadow made tender,
> Till love falls asleep in its sameness of splendor."

We would infinitely prefer to nurse a sickly woman, to being led about by a masculine blue stocking. Mrs. Boswell complained that her husband, following Dr. Johnson, resembled a man led about by a bear. We would rather be led by a bear than a woman. He looks more formidable and master-like.

To the husbands of pedantic, masculine women, the lines of Byron may be well applied—

> "But oh! ye Lords of ladies intellectual,
> Inform us truly, have they not hen-pecked you all."

As we are in the poetic vein, and this chapter is intended solely for the eyes of the ladies, all of whom love poetry, (though none of them can

K

write it,) we will quote a whole ode of Schiller, which expresses our thoughts on this subject far better than we can express them ourselves. Poetry and painting require boldness, originality and inventiveness. The ladies are too modest to practise these qualities, and only become coarse when they attempt to be bold. Sappho is an exception, but Sappho, we suspect, was a Myth or a man. We offer this beautiful ode to the ladies as a propitiation for all the wicked things we have said about them:

HONOR TO WOMAN.

Honor to Woman! To her it is given
To guard the earth with the roses of heaven !
   All blessed, she linketh the Loves in their choir;
In the veil of the Graces her beauty concealing,
She tends on each altar that's hallowed to Feeling
   And keeps ever living the fire !

    From the bounds of truth careering,
      Man's strong spirit wildly sweeps,
    With each hasty impulse veering
      Down to Passion's troubled deeps.
    And his heart contented never,
      Goads to grapple with the far,
    Chasing his own dream forever,
      On through many a distant star !

But Woman, with looks that can charm and enchain,
Lureth back at her beck the wild truant again,
   By the spell of her presence beguiled;
In the home of the mother, her modest abode,
And modest the manners by Nature bestowed
   On Nature's most exquisite child !

Bruised and worn, but fiercely breasting,
  Foe to foe, the angry strife;
Man, the wild one, never resting,
  Braves along the troubled life;
What he planneth, still pursuing;
  Vainly as the hydra bleeds.
Crest the severed crest renewing—
  Wish to withered wish succeeds.

But woman, at peace with all being, reposes,
And seeks from the moment to gather the roses,
  Whose sweets to her culture belong.
Ah! richer than he, though his soul reigneth o'er
The mighty dominion of Genius and Love,
  And the infinite Circle of Song.

Strong and proud and self-depending,
  Man's cold bosom beats alone;
Heart with heart divinely blending
  In the love that gods have known,
Soul's sweet interchange of feeling,
  Melting tears—he never knows.
Each hard sense, the hard one steeling,
  Arms against a world of foes.

Alive, as the wind harp, how lightly soever
If woo'd by the Zephyr, to music will quiver,
  Is woman to Hope and to Fear;
Ah! tender one! still at the shadow of grieving,
How quiver the chords—how thy bosom is heaving—
  How trembles thy glance through the tear!

Man's dominion, war and labor:
  Might to right the statute gave;
Laws are in the Scythian's sabre;
  Where the Mede reign'd—see the slave!
Peace and meekness grimly routing,
  Prowl's the War-lust, rude and wild;
Eris rages, hoarsely shouting,
  Where the vanished Graces smiled.

But Woman, the Soft One, persuasively prayeth,
Of the life that she charmeth, the sceptre she swayeth;
   She lulls, as she looks from above,
The Discord whose hell for its victims is gaping,
And blending awhile, then forever escaping,
   Whispers Hate to the image of Love!

CHAPTER XXVIII.

THE SUMMING UP.

" Why, my dear Lucifer, would you abuse
My call for witnesses ?   I did not mean
That you should half of earth and hell produce ;
'Tis even superfluous, since two honest, clean,
True testimonies are enough : We live
Our time, nay, our eternity, between
The accusation and defence : if we
Hear both, 'twill stretch our immortality."

The Vision of Judgment.

We did not intend to write the history of slavery, or to treat of it in all its aspects. It has been so interwoven with all the relations and history of human kind, that to do so would require a Moral Cosmos and a history of the world.   Our chief object has been to prove the failure of free society. We knew if we succeeded in that, the various theories propounded in this work on other subjects would be found, when closely examined, necessary results, or legitimate sequences.

In order to enable the reader fully to comprehend our argument, and to furnish a fair field for its refutation, if false, we will now sum up the chief points which we have made, and on which we rely.

First. Free society is theoretically impracticable, because its friends admit that "in all old countries the supply of labor exceeds the demand." Hence a part of the laboring class must be out of employment and starving, and in their struggle to get employment, reducing those next above them to the minimum that will support human existence.

Secondly. The late invention and use of the word Sociology in free society, and of the science of which it treats, and the absence of such word and science in slave society, shows that the former is afflicted with disease, the latter healthy.

Thirdly. We prove the failure, from history and statistics.

Fourthly. We prove it from the exodus now going on from Western Europe with all the reckless panic and trepidation of a " Sauve que peut ! "

And, lastly, we prove it from the universal admission of all writers who have of late years treated of the subject of society in Free Europe.

For thirty years the South has been a field on which abolitionists, foreign and domestic, have carried on offensive warfare. Let us now, in turn, act on the offensive, transfer the seat of war, and invade the enemy's territory.

APPENDIX.

APPENDIX.

Our little work has by untoward circumstances been delayed in its publication. Ten years ago we became satisfied that slavery, *black or white*, was right and necessary. We advocated this doctrine in very many essays; sometimes editorially and sometimes as a communicant. The *Fredericksburg Recorder* and *Richmond Examiner* will testify to this fact. We republish in this Appendix a series of essays that first appeared in the *Democratic Recorder*, of Fredericksburg, in 1849, 1850, and 1851.

Few papers in the Union then had the stern courage and integrity to admit such articles into their columns. We then published them in pamphlet form, for a few friends. We now re-publish them, because, whatever " bad eminence " we may attain from being the first to write the *Justification and Philosophy of Slavery*, we prefer that position to being considered the mere follower in the wake of evil doers. We believe we are morally and religiously right. We know that if wrong, we can be easily confuted.

SLAVERY JUSTIFIED.

Liberty and equality are new things under the sun.
The free states of antiquity abounded with slaves.
The feudal system that supplanted Roman institutions
changed the form of slavery, but brought with it neither
liberty nor equality. France and the Northern States of
our Union have alone fully and fairly tried the experiment of a social organization founded upon universal
liberty and equality of rights. England has only approximated to this condition in her commercial and
manufacturing cities. The examples of small communities in Europe are not fit exponents of the working of
the system. In France and in our Northern States the
experiment has already failed, if we are to form our
opinions from the discontent of the masses, or to believe
the evidence of the Socialists, Communists, Anti-Renters,
and a thousand other agrarian sects that have arisen
in these countries, and threaten to subvert the whole social fabric. The leaders of these sects, at least in France,
comprise within their ranks the greater number of the
most cultivated and profound minds in the nation, who
have made government their study. Add to the evidence
of these social philosophers, who, watching closely the
working of the system, have proclaimed to the world its
total failure, the condition of the working classes, and we

have conclusive proof that liberty and equality have not conduced to enhance the comfort or the happiness of the people. Crime and pauperism have increased. Riots, trades unions, strikes for higher wages, discontent breaking out into revolution, are things of daily occurrence, and show that the poor see and feel quite as clearly as the philosophers, that their condition is far worse under the new than under the old order of things. Radicalism and Chartism in England owe their birth to the free and equal institutions of her commercial and manufacturing districts, and are little heard of in the quiet farming districts, where remnants of feudalism still exist in the relation of landlord and tenant, and in the laws of entail and primogeniture.

So much for experiment. We will now endeavor to treat the subject theoretically, and to show that the system is on its face self-destructive and impracticable. When we look to the vegetable, animal and human kingdoms, we discover in them all a constant conflict, war, or race of competition, the result of which is, that the weaker or less healthy genera, species and individuals are continually displaced and exterminated by the stronger and more hardy. It is a means by which some contend Nature is perfecting her own work. We, however, witness the war, but do not see the improvement. Although from the earliest date of recorded history, one race of plants has been eating out and taking the place of another, the stronger or more cunning animals been destroying the feebler, and man exterminating and supplanting his fellow, still the plants, the animals and the men of to-day seem not at all superior, even in those qualities of strength and hardihood to which they owe their continued existence, to those of thousands of years ago. To this propensity of the strong to oppress and destroy the weak, government owes its existence. So strong is this propensity, and so destructive to human existence, that man has never yet been found so savage as to be without government. Forgetful of this important fact, which is the origin of all governments, the political economists and the advocates of liberty and equality propose to enhance the well being of man by trammeling his conduct as little as possible, and encouraging what they call FREE COMPETITION. Now, free competition is but another name for liberty and equality, and we must acquire precise and accurate notions about it in order to ascertain how free institutions will work. It is, then, that war or conflict to which Nature impels her creatures, and which government was intended to restrict. It is true, it is that war somewhat modified and restricted, for the warmest friends of freedom would have some government. The question is, whether the proposed restrictions are sufficient to neutralize the self-destructive tendencies which nature impresses on society. We proceed to show that the war of the wits, of mind with mind, which free competition or liberty and equality beget and encourage, is quite as oppressive, cruel and exterminating, as the war of the sword, of theft, robbery, and murder, which it forbids. It is only substituting strength of mind for strength of body. Men are told it is their duty to compete, to endeavor to get ahead of and supplant their fellow men, by the exercise of all the intellectual and moral strength with which nature and education have endowed them. "Might makes right," is the order of creation, and this law of nature, so far as mental might is concerned, is restored by liberty to man. The struggle to better one's condition, to pull others down or supplant them, is the great organic law of free society. All men being equal, all aspire to the highest honors and the largest possessions. Good men and bad men teach their children one and the same lesson—"Go ahead, push your way in the world." In such society, virtue, if virtue there be, loses all her loveliness because of her selfish aims. None but the selfish virtues are encouraged, because none other aid a-man in the race of free competition. Good men and bad men have the same end in view, are in pursuit of the same object—self-promotion, self-elevation. The good man is prudent, cautious, and cunning of fence ; he knows well the arts (the virtues, if you please,) which will advance his fortunes and enable him to depress and supplant others; he bides his time, takes advantage of the follies, the improvidence, and vices of others, and makes his fortune out of the misfortunes of his fellow men. The bad man is rash, hasty, and unskillful. He is equally selfish, but not half so cunning. Selfishness is almost the only motive of human conduct with good and bad in free society, where every man is taught that he may change and better his condition. A vulgar adage, "Every man for himself, and devil take the hindmost," is the moral which liberty and free competition inculcate. Now, there are no more honors and wealth in proportion to numbers, in this generation, than in the one which preceded it; population fully keeps pace with the means of subsistence; hence, these who better their condition or rise to higher places in society, do so generally by pulling down others or pushing them from their places. Where men of strong minds, of strong wills, and of great self-control, come into free competition with the weak and improvident, the latter soon become the inmates of jails and penitentiaries.

The statistics of France, England and America show that pauperism and crime advance *pari passu* with liberty and equality. How can it be otherwise, when all society is combined to oppress the poor and weak minded? The rich man, however good he may be, employs the laborer who will work for the least wages. If he be a good man, his punctuality enables him to cheapen the wages of the poor man. The poor war with one another in the race of competition, in order to get employment, by underbidding; for laborers are more abundant than employers. Population increases faster than capital. Look to the situation of woman when she is thrown into this war of competition, and has to support herself by her daily wages. For the same or equally valuable services she gets not half the pay that man does, simply because the modesty of her sex prevents her from resorting to all the arts and means of competition which men employ. He who would emancipate woman, unless he could make her as coarse and strong in mind and body as man, would be her worst enemy; her subservience to and dependence on man, is necessary to her very existence. She is not a soldier fitted to enlist in the war of free competition. We do not set children and women free because they are not capable of taking care of themselves, not equal to the constant struggle of society. To set them free would be to give the lamb to the wolf to take care of. Society would quickly devour them. If the children of ten years of age were remitted to all the rights of person and property which men enjoy, all can perceive how soon ruin and penury would overtake them. But half of mankind are but grown-up children, and liberty is as fatal to them as it would be to children.

We will cite another familiar instance to prove and illustrate the destructive effects of liberty or free competition. It is that where two races of men of different capacity are brought into juxtaposition. It is the boast of the Anglo-Saxon, that by the arts of peace under the influence of free trade he can march to universal conquest. However true this may be, all know that if Englishmen or Americans settle among inferior races, they soon become the owners of the soil, and gradually extirpate or reduce to poverty the original owners. They are the wire-grass of nations. The same law of nature which enables and impels the stronger race to oppress and exterminate the weaker, is constantly at work in the bosom of every society, between its stronger and weaker members. Liberty and equality rather encourage than restrict this law in its deadly operation. A Northern gentleman, who was both statesman and philosopher, once told us, that his only objection to domestic slavery was, that it would perpetuate an inferior race, who, under the influence of free trade and free competition, would otherwise disappear from the earth. China and Japan acted wisely to anticipate this new philosophy and exclude Europeans.*

One step more, and that the most difficult in this process of reasoning and illustration, and we have done with this part of our subject. Liberty and equality throw the whole weight of society on its weakest members; they combine all men in oppressing precisely that part of mankind who most need sympathy, aid and protection. The very astute and avaricious man, when left free to exercise his faculties, is injured by no one in the field of competition, but levies a tax on all with whom he deals. The sensible and prudent, but less astute man, is seldom worsted in competing with his fellow men, and generally benefited. The very simple and improvident man is the prey of every body. The simple man represents a class, the common day laborers. The employer cheapens their wages, and the retail dealer takes advantage of their ignorance, their inability to visit other markets, and their want of credit, to charge them enormous profits. They bear the whole weight of society on their shoulders; they are the producers and artificers of all the necessaries, the comforts, the luxuries, the pomp and splendor of the world; they create it all, and enjoy none of it; they are the muzzled ox that treadeth out the straw; they are at constant war with those above them, asking higher wages but getting lower; for they are also at war with each other, underbidding to get employment. This process of underbidding never ceases so long as employ-

---

* But free trade has conquered. Chinese are shipped off as slaves, and Japan trembles as she hears the knocking at her door.

ers want profits or laborers want employment. It ends when wages are reduced too low to afford subsistence, in filling poor-houses, and jails, and graves. It has reached that point already in France, England and Ireland. A half million died of hunger in one year in Ireland—they died because in the eye of the law they were the equals, and liberty had made them the enemies, of their landlords and employers. Had they been vassals or serfs, they would have been beloved, cherished and taken care of by those same landlords and employers. Slaves never die of hunger, scarcely ever feel want.

The bestowing upon men equality of rights, is but giving license to the strong to oppress the weak. It begets the grossest inequalities of condition. Menials and day laborers are and must be as numerous as in a land of slavery. And these menials and laborers are only taken care of while young, strong and healthy. If the laborer gets sick, his wages cease just as his demands are greatest. If two of the poor get married, who being young and healthy, are getting good wages, in a few years they may have four children. Their wants have increased, but the mother has enough to do to nurse the four children, and the wages of the husband must support six. There is no equality, except in theory, in such society, and there is no liberty. The men of property, those who own lands and money, are masters of the poor; masters, with none of the feelings, interests or sympathies of masters; they employ them when they please, and for what they please, and may leave them to die in the highway, for it is the only home to which the poor in free countries are entitled. They (the property holders)

beheaded Charles Stuart and Louis Capet, because these
kings asserted a divine right to govern wrong, and forgot
that office was a trust to be exercised for the benefit of
the governed; and yet they seem to think that property
is of divine right, and that they may abuse its possession
to the detriment of the rest of society, as much as they
please. A pretty exchange the world would make, to
get rid of kings who often love and protect the poor, and
get in their place a million of pelting, petty officers in
the garb of money-changers and land-owners, who think
that as they own all the property, the rest of mankind
have no right to a living, except on the conditions they
may prescribe. "'Tis bettter to fall before the lion than
the wolf," and modern liberty has substituted a thousand
wolves for a few lions. The vulgar landlords, capitalists
and employers of to-day, have the liberties and lives of
the people more completely in their hands, than had the
kings, barons and gentlemen of former times; and they
hate and oppress the people as cordially as the people
despise them. But these vulgar parvenus, these psalm-
singing regicides, these worshipers of mammon, "have
but taught bloody instructions, which being taught, return to plague the inventor." The king's office was a
trust, so are your lands, houses and money. Society permits you to hold them, because private property well
administered conduces to the good of all society. *This
is your only title;* you lose your right to your property,
as the king did to his crown, so soon as you cease faithfully to execute your trust; you can't make commons
and forests of your lands and starve mankind; you must
manage your lands to produce the most food and raiment

for mankind, or you forfeit your title ; you may not understand this philosophy, but you feel that it is true, and
are trembling in your seats as you hear the murmurings
and threats of the starving poor.

The moral effect of free society is to banish Christian
virtue, that virtue which bids us love our neighbor as
ourself, and to substitute the very equivocal virtues proceeding from mere selfishness. The intense struggle to
better each one's pecuniary condition, the rivalries, the
jealousies, the hostilities which it begets, leave neither
time nor inclination to cultivate the heart or the head.
Every finer feeling of our nature is chilled and benumbed
by its selfish atmosphere ; affection is under the ban,
because affection makes us less regardful of mere self ;
hospitality is considered criminal waste, chivalry a stum-
bling-block, and the code of honor foolishness ; taste,
sentiment, imagination, are forbidden ground, because
no money is to be made by them. Gorgeous pageantry
and sensual luxury are the only pleasures indulged in,
because they alone are understood and appreciated, and
they are appreciated just for what they cost in dollars
and cents. What makes money, and what costs money,
are alone desired. Temperance, frugality, thrift, attention to business, industry, and skill in making bargains)
are virtues in high repute, because they enable us to supplant others and increase our own wealth. The character of our Northern brethren, and of the Dutch, is proof
enough of the justice of these reflections. The Puritan
fathers had lived in Holland, and probably imported
Norway rats and Dutch morality in the Mayflower.

Liberty and equality are not only destructive to the morals, but to the happiness of society. Foreigners have all remarked on the care-worn, thoughtful, unhappy countenances of our people, and the remark only applies to the North, for travellers see little of us at the South, who live far from highways and cities, in contentment on our farms.

The facility with which men may improve their condition would, indeed, be a consideration much in favor of free society, if it did not involve as a necessary consequence the equal facility and liability to lose grade and fortune. As many fall as rise. The wealth of society hardly keeps pace with its numbers. All cannot be rich. The rich and the poor change places oftener than where there are fixed hereditary distinctions; so often, that the sense of insecurity makes every one unhappy; so often, that we see men clutching at security through means of Odd Fellows, Temperance Societies, &c., which provide for members when sick, and for the families of deceased members; so often, that almost every State in the Union has of late years enacted laws or countenanced decisions giving more permanency to property. Entails and primogeniture are as odious to us as kings were to the Romans; but their object—to keep property in our families—is as dear to us as to any people on earth, because we love our families as much. Hence laws to exempt small amounts of personal property from liability to debt are daily enacted, and hence Iowa or Wisconsin has a provision in her constitution, that the homestead of some forty acres shall be exempt from execution. Hence, also, the mighty impulse of late in favor of woman's rights. Legislatures and courts are vieing with each other which shall do most to secure married women's rights to them. The ruin of thousands upon thousands of families in the revulsion of 1837, taught the necessity of this new species of entail, this new way of keeping property in the family. The ups and downs of life became too rapid to be agreeable to any who had property to lose or a family to provide for. We have not yet quite cooled down from the fervor of the Revolution. We have been looking to one side only of our institutions. We begin to feel, however, that there is another and a dark side,—a side where all are seen going down the hill of fortune. Let us look closely and fearlessly at this feature of free society, so much lauded and so little understood. What object more laudable, what so dear to a man's heart, as to continue a competency of property, refinement of mind and morals, to his posterity? What nobler incentive to virtuous conduct, than the belief that such conduct will redound to the advantage of our descendants? What reflection so calculated to make men reckless, wretched and immoral, as the conviction that the means they employ to improve the moral, mental and pecuniary condition of their offspring, are, in this land of ups and downs, the very means to make them the prey of the cunning, avaricious and unprincipled, who have been taught in the school of adversity and poverty? We constantly boast that the wealthy and powerful of to-day are the sons of the weak, ignorant and destitute of yesterday. It is the other side of the picture that we want moral courage to look at. We are dealing now with figures of arithmetic, not of rhetoric.

Those who rise, pull down a class as numerous, and often more worthy than themselves, to the abyss of misery and penury. Painful as it may be, the reader shall look with us at this dark side of the picture; he shall view the vanquished as well as the victors on this battle-ground of competition; he shall see those who were delicately reared, taught no tricks of trade, no shifts of thrifty avarice, spurned, insulted, down-trodden by the coarse and vulgar, whose wits and whose appetites had been sharpened by necessity. If he can sympathize with fallen virtue or detest successful vice, he will see nothing in this picture to admire.

The wide fields of the newly rich will cease to excite pleasure in the contemplation; they will look like Golgothas covered with human bones. Their coarse and boisterous joys, while they revel in their spoils, will not help to relieve the painful sympathies for their victims.

But these parvenus are men with all the feelings of men, though somewhat blunted by the race for wealth; they love their children, and would have them unlike themselves, moral, refined, and educated—above the necessities and tricks of their parents. They rear them as gentlemen, to become the victims in their turn of the children of fallen gentlemen of a past generation—these latter having learned in the school of adversity the path to fortune. In Heaven's name, what is human life worth with such prospects ahead? Who would not rather lie down and die than exert himself to educate and make fortunes for his children, when he has reason to fear that by so doing he is to heap coals of fire on their heads. And yet this is an exact picture of the prospect which universal liberty holds out to its votaries. It is true it hides with a veil the agonies of the vanquished, and only exhibits the vulgar mirth of the victors. We have lifted the veil.

In Boston, a city famed for its wealth and the prudence of its inhabitants, nine-tenths of the men in business fail. In the slaveholding South, except in new settlements, failures are extremely rare; small properties descend from generation to generation in the same family; there is as much stability and permanency of property as is compatible with energy and activity in society; fortunes are made rather by virtuous industry than by tricks, cunning and speculation.

We have thus attempted to prove from theory and from actual experiment that a society of universal liberty and equality is absurd and impracticable. We have performed our task, we know, indifferently, but hope we have furnished suggestions that may be profitably used by those more accustomed to authorship.

We now come in the order of our subject to treat of the various new sects of philosophers that have appeared of late years in France and in our free States, who, disgusted with society as it exists, propose to re-organize it on entirely new principles. We have never heard of a convert to any of these theories in the slave States. If we are not all contented, still none see evils of such magnitude in society as to require its entire subversion and reconstruction. We shall group all these sects together, because they all concur in the great truth that Free Competition is the bane of free society; they all concur, too, in modifying or wholly destroying the institution of private property. Many of them, seeing that property enables its owners to exercise a more grinding oppression than kings ever did, would destroy its tenure altogether. In France, especially, these sects are headed by men of great ability, who saw the experiment of liberty and equality fairly tested in France after the revolution of 1792. They saw, as all the world did, that it failed to promote human happiness or well-being.

France found the Consulate and the Empire havens of bliss compared with the stormy ocean of liberty and equality on which she had been tossed. Wise, however, as these Socialists and Communists of France are, they cannot create a man, a tree, or a new system of society; these are God's works, which man may train, trim and modify, but cannot create. The attempt to establish government on purely theoretical abstract speculation, regardless of circumstance and experience, has always failed; never more signally than with the Socialists.

The frequent experience of the Abbe Sieye's paper structures of government, which lasted so short a time, should have taught them caution; but they were bolder reformers than he; they had a fair field for their experiment after the expulsion of Louis Phillippe; they tried it, and their failure was complete and ridiculous. The Abbe's structures were adamant compared to theirs. The rule of the weak Louis Napoleon was welcomed as a fortunate escape from their schemes of universal benevolence, which issued in universal bankruptcy.

The sufferings of the Irish, and the complaints of the Radicals and Chartists, have given birth to a new party in England, called Young England. This party saw in

the estrangement and hostility of classes, and the sufferings of the poor, the same evils of free competition that
had given rise to Socialism in France; though less tal-
ented than the Socialists, they came much nearer discov-
ering the remedy for these evils.

Young England belongs to the most conservative wing
of the tory party; he inculcates strict subordination of
rank; would have the employer kind, attentive and paternal, in his treatment of the operative. The operative,
humble, affectionate and obedient to his employer. He
is young, and sentimental, and would spread his doctrines
in tracts, sonnets and novels; but society must be ruled
by sterner stuff than sentiment. Self-interest makes the
employer and free laborer enemies. The one prefers to
pay low wages, the other needs high wages. War, constant war, is the result, in which the operative perishes,
but is not vanquished; he is hydra-headed, and when he
dies two take his place. But numbers diminish his
strength. The competition among laborers to get employment begets an intestine war, more destructive than
the war from above. There is but one remedy for this
evil, so inherent in free society, and that is, to identify
the interests of the weak and the strong, the poor and
the rich. Domestic Slavery does this far better than
any other institution. Feudalism only answered the
purpose in so far as Feudalism retained the features of
slavery. To it (slavery) Greece and Rome, Egypt and
Judea, and all the other distinguished States of antiquity, were indebted for their great prosperity and high
civilization; a prosperity and a civilization which appear
almost miraculous, when we look to their ignorance of

the physical sciences. In the moral sciences they were our equals, in the fine arts vastly our superiors. Their poetry, their painting, their sculpture, their drama, their elocution, and their architecture, are models which we imitate, but never equal. In the science of government and of morals, in pure metaphysics, and in all the walks of intellectual philosophy, we have been beating the air with our wings or revolving in circles, but have not advanced an inch. Kant is not ahead of Aristotle—and Juvenal has expressed in little more than a line the modern utilitarian morality—

> Quis enim virtutem amplectitur ipsam
> Prœmia si tollas ?

Terence, himself a slave, with a heart no doubt filled with the kindly affections which the relation of master and slave begets, uttered the loftiest sentiment that ever emanated from uninspired man :

> Homo sum ; humani nihil a me alienum puto.*

But this high civilization and domestic slavery did not merely co-exist, they were cause and effect. Every scholar whose mind is at all imbued with ancient history and literature, sees that Greece and Rome were indebted to this institution alone for the taste, the leisure and the means to cultivate their heads and their hearts ; had they been tied down to Yankee notions of thrift, they might have produced a Franklin, with his " penny saved is a penny gained ; " they might have had utilitarian philos-

---

* The line and a half from Juvenal expresses the philosophy and moralé of free society : that from Terence the moral of slave society.

ophers and invented the spinning jenny, but they never would have produced a poet, an orator, a sculptor or an architect; they would never have uttered a lofty sentiment, achieved a glorious feat in war, or created a single work of art.

A modern Yankee, or a Dutchman, is the fair result of liberty and equality. French character has not yet been subdued and tamed into insignificance by their new institutions; and besides, the pursuit of arms elevates and purifies the sentiments of Frenchmen. In what is the Yankee or Dutchman comparable to the Roman, Athenian or Spartan? In nothing save his care of his pelf and his skill in driving a bargain. The ruins of Thebes, of Nineveh, and of Balbec, the obelisks and pyramids of Egypt, the lovely and time-defying relics of Roman and Grecian art, the Doric column and the Gothic spire, alike attest the taste, the genius and the energy of society where slavery existed.

> Quis locus,
> Quœ regio in terris non nostri plena laboris?

And now Equality where are thy monuments? And Echo answers where! Echo deep, deep, from the bowels of the earth, where women and children drag out their lives in darkness, harnessed like horses to heavy cars loaded with ore. Or, perhaps, it is an echo from some grand, gloomy and monotonous factory, where pallid children work fourteen hours a day, and go home at night to sleep in damp cellars. It may be too, this cellar contains aged parents too old to work, and cast off by their employer to die. Great railroads and mighty steamships too, thou mayest boast, but still the operatives who construct them are beings destined to poverty and neglect. Not a vestige of art canst thou boast; not a ray of genius illumes thy handiwork. The sordid spirit of mammon presides o'er all, and from all proceed the sighs and groans of the oppressed.

Domestic slavery in the Southern States has produced the same results in elevating the character of the master that it did in Greece and Rome. | He is lofty and independent in his sentiments, generous, affectionate, brave and eloquent; he is superior to the Northerner in every thing but the arts of thrift. History proves this. A Yankee sometimes gets hold of the reins of State, attempts Apollo, but acts Phæton. Scipio and Aristides, Calhoun and Washington, are the noble results of domestic slavery. Like Egyptian obelisks 'mid the waste of time—simple, severe, sublime,— they point ever heavenward, and lift the soul by their examples. Adams and Van Buren, cunning, complex and tortuous, are fit exponents of the selfish system of universal liberty.* Coriolanus, marching to the gates of Rome with dire hate and deadly indignation, is grand and noble in his revenge. Adams and Van Buren, insidiously striking with reptile fangs at the South, excite in all bosoms hatred and contempt; but we will not indulge in sweeping denunciation. In public and in private life, the North has many noble and generous souls. Men who,

---

*The North was pushing the Wilmot Proviso when this was written. We wrote under angry excitement. We did Mr. Van Buren injustice and the North injustice. We believe Mr. Van Buren thoroughly patriotic, though wrong on the Proviso; and we think Northerners more fanatical than selfish.

like Webster and Cass, Dickinson and Winthrop,* can soar in lofty eloquence beyond the narrow prejudices of time and place, see man in all his relations, and contemn the narrow morality which makes the performance of one duty the excuse for a thousand crimes. We speak only of the usual and common effects of slavery and of equality. The Turk, half civilized as he is, exhibits the manly, noble and generous traits of character peculiar to the slave owner; he is hospitable, generous, truthful, brave, and strictly honest. In many respects, he is the finest specimen of humanity to be found in the world.

But the chief and far most important enquiry is, how does slavery affect the condition of the slave? One of the wildest sects of Communists in France proposes not only to hold all property in common, but to divide the profits, not according to each man's in-put and labor, but according to each man's wants. Now this is precisely the system of domestic slavery with us. We provide for each slave, in old age and in infancy, in sickness and in health, not according to his labor, but according to his wants. The master's wants are more costly and refined, and he therefore gets a larger share of the profits. A Southern farm is the beau ideal of Communism; it is a joint concern, in which the slave consumes more than the master, of the coarse products, and is far happier, because although the concern may fail, he is always sure of a support; he is only transferred to another master to participate in the profits of

---

*We had not seen Mr. Winthrop's late speech when this was written.

another concern; he marries when he pleases, because
he knows he will have to work no more with a family
than without one, and whether he live or die, that family
will be taken care of; he exhibits all the pride of ownership, despises a partner in a smaller concern, "a
poor man's negro," boasts of "our crops, horses,
fields and cattle;" and is as happy as a human being
can be. And why should he not?—he enjoys as much
of the fruits of the farm as he is capable of doing, and
the wealthiest can do no more. Great wealth brings
many additional cares, but few additional enjoyments.
Our stomachs do not increase in capacity with our fortunes. We want no more clothing to keep us warm.
We may create new wants, but we cannot create new
pleasures. The intellectual enjoyments which wealth
affords are probably balanced by the new cares it brings
along with it.

  There is no rivalry, no competition to get employment
among slaves, as among free laborers. Nor is there a
war between master and slave. The master's interest
prevents his reducing the slave's allowance or wages in
infancy or sickness, for he might lose the slave by so
doing. His feeling for his slave never permits him to
stint him in old age. The slaves are all well fed, well
clad, have plenty of fuel, and are happy. They have
no dread of the future—no fear of want. A state of
dependence is the only condition in which reciprocal
affection can exist among human beings—the only
situation in which the war of competition ceases, and
peace, amity and good will arise. A state of independence always begets more or less of jealous rivalry and
hostility. A man loves his children because they are

weak, helpless and dependent; he loves his wife for similar reasons. When his children grow. up and assert their independence, he is apt to transfer his affection to his grand-children. He ceases to love his wife when she becomes masculine or rebellious; but slaves are always dependent, never the rivals of their master. Hence, though men are often found at variance with wife or children, we never saw one who did not like his slaves, and rarely a slave who was not devoted to his master. "I am thy servant!" disarms me of the power of master. Every man feels the beauty, force and truth of. this sentiment of Sterne. But he who acknowledges its truth, tacitly admits that dependence is a tie of affection, that the relation of master and slave is one of mutual good will. Volumes written on the subject would not prove as much as this single sentiment. It has found its way to the heart of every reader, and carried conviction along with it. The slaveholder is like other men; he will not tread on the worm nor break the bruised reed. The ready submission of the slave, nine times out of ten, disarms his wrath even when the slave has offended. The habit of command may make him imperious and fit him for rule; but he is only imperious when thwarted or crossed by his equals; he would scorn to put on airs of command among blacks, whether slaves or free; he always speaks to them in a kind and subdued tone. We go farther, and say the slave-holder is better than others—because he has greater occasion for the exercise of the affections. His whole life is spent in providing for the minutest wants of others, in taking care of them in sickness and in health. Hence he is the least selfish of men. Is not the old bachelor who retires to seclusion, always selfish? Is not the head of a large family almost always kind and benevolent? And is not the slave-holder the head of the largest family? Nature compels master and slave to be friends; nature makes employers and free laborers enemies.

The institution of slavery gives full development and full play to the affections. Free society chills, stints and eradicates them. In a homely way the farm will support all, and we are not in a hurry to send our children into the world, to push their way and make their fortunes, with a capital of knavish maxims. We are better husbands, better fathers, better friends, and better neighbors than our Northern brethren. The tie of kindred to the fifth degree is often a tie of affection with us. First cousins are scarcely acknowledged at the North, and even children are prematurely pushed off into the world. Love for others is the organic law of our society, as self-love is of theirs.

Every social structure must have its substratum. In free society this substratum, the weak, poor and ignorant, is borne down upon and oppressed with continually increasing weight by all above. We have solved the problem of relieving this substratum from the pressure from above. The slaves are the substratum, and the master's feelings and interests alike prevent him from bearing down upon and oppressing them. With us the pressure on society is like that of air or water, so equally diffused as not any where to be felt. With them it is the pressure of the enormous screw, never yielding, continually increasing. Free laborers are little better than trespassers on this earth given by God to all mankind. The birds of the air have nests, and the foxes have holes, but they have not where to lay their heads. They are driven to cities to dwell in damp and crowded cellars, and thousands are even forced to lie in the open air. This accounts for the rapid growth of Northern cities. The feudal Barons were more generous and hospitable and less tyrannical than the petty land-holders- of modern times. Besides, each inhabitant of the barony was considered as having some right of residence, some claim to protection from the Lord of the Manor. A few of them escaped to the municipalities for purposes of trade, and to enjoy a larger liberty. Now penury and the want of a home drive thousands to towns. The slave always has a home, always an interest in the proceeds of the soil.

An intelligent New Englander, who was much opposed to negro slavery, boasting of his own country, told us that native New Englanders rarely occupied the place of domestic or body servants, or that of hired day laborers on public works. Emigrants alone served as menials, cleansed the streets, and worked on railroads and canals. New England is busy importing white free laborers for the home market, and catching negroes in Africa for the Brazilian market. Some of the negroes die on the passage, but few after they arrive in Brazil. The masters can't afford to neglect them. Many of the white laborers die on the passage of cholera and other diseases occasioned by filth and crowding—a fourth of them probably in the first year after they arrive, for the want of employment or the neglect of employers. The horrors of the middle passage are nothing to the horrors of a deck passage up the Mississippi when cholera prevails, or the want, penury and exposure that emigrants are subjected to in our large cities. England, too, has a tender conscience about slavery, but she is importing captured African slaves into her colonies to serve as apprentices, and extending this new species of slave trade even to Asia. "Expel nature with a fork, she will soon return." Slavery is natural and necessary, and will in some form insinuate itself into all civilized society.— The domestic slave trade is complained of, and justly too, because it severs family ties. It is one of the evils of slavery, and no institution is without its evils. But how is it with New England? Are none of the free, the delicately reared and enlightened forced to quit the domestic hearth and all its endearments, to seek a living among strangers? Delicacy forbids our dwelling on this painful topic. The instances are before our eyes. What would induce a Virginian, rich or poor, to launch such members of his family unattended on the cold world.

More than half of the white citizens of the North are common laborers, either in the field, or as body or house servants. They perform the same services that our slaves do. They serve their employers for hire; they have quite as little option whether they shall so serve, or not, as our slaves, for they cannot live without their wages. Their hire or wages, except with the healthy and able-bodied, are not half what we allow our slaves, for it is wholly insufficient for their comfortable maintenance, whilst we always keep our slaves in comfort, in return for their past, present, or expected labor. The socialists say wages is slavery. It is a gross libel on slavery. Wages are given in time of vigorous health and strength, and denied when most needed, when sickness or old age has overtaken us. The slave is never without a master to maintain him. The free laborer, though willing to work, cannot always find an employer. He is then without a home and without wages! In a densely peopled country, where the supply of laborers exceeds the demand, wages is worse than slavery. Oh! Liberty and Equality, to what a sad pass do you bring your votaries! This is the exact condition to which the mass of society is reduced in France and England, and to which it is rapidly approximating in our Northern States. This state of things brought about the late revolution in France. The Socialist rulers undertook to find employment, put the laborers of Paris to work, transplanting trees and digging the earth. This experiment worked admirably in all but one respect. The government could find employment, but could not find wages. THE RIGHT TO EMPLOYMENT! Frenchmen deluged Paris with fraternal gore to vindicate this right. The right to live when you are strong enough to work, for it is then only you want employment. Poor as this boon would be, it is one which Liberty and Equality cannot confer. If it were conferred, the free laborer's condition would still be below

the slave's, for the wages of the slave are paid whether
he is fit for employment or not.

> Oh carry, carry me back to old Virginia shore,
> For I am old and feeble grown,
> And cannot work any more.

Liberty and Equality, thou art humble in thy preten-
sions; thou askest little. But that little inexorable
fate denies thee. Literally and truly, "darkness,
death and black despair surround thee."

In France, England, Scotland and Ireland, the genius of famine hovers o'er the land. Emigrants, like a
flock of hungry pigeons or Egyptian locusts, are alight-
ng on the North. Every green thing will soon be
iconsumed. The hollow, bloated prosperity which she
now enjoys is destined soon to pass away. Her wealth
does not increase with her numbers; she is dependent
for the very necessaries of life on the slaveholding
States. If those States cut off commercial intercourse
with her, as they certainly will do if she does not
speedily cease interference with slavery, she will be
without food or clothing for her overgrown population.
She is already threatened with a social revolution. The
right to separate property in land is not only questioned
by many, but has been successfully denied in the case
of the Anti-Renters. Judges and Governors are elected
upon pledges that they will sustain those who deny this
right and defy the law. The editor of the most influential paper in the North, lately a member of Congress,
is carrying on open war, not only against the right of
property, but against every institution held sacred by

society. A people who can countenance and patronise such doctrines, are almost ripe to carry those doctrines into practice. An insurrection of the poor against the rich may happen speedily among them. Should it occur, they have no means of suppressing it. No standing army, no efficient militia, no strength in their State governments. Society is hurrying on to the gulf of agrarianism, and no port of safety is in sight; no remedy for the evils with which it is beset has been suggested, save the remedies of the Socialists; remedies tried in France and proved to be worthless. Population is too dense to introduce negro slaves. White men will not submit to be slaves, and are not fitted for slavery if they would. To the European race some degree of liberty is necessary, though famine stare them in the face. We are informed in Holy Writ, that God ordained certain races of men for slaves. The wisest philosopher of ancient times, with the experience of slavery before his eyes, proclaimed the same truth. Modern Abolitionists, wiser than Moses and Aristotle, have discovered that all men should be free. They have yet to discover the means of sustaining their lives in a state of freedom.

At the slaveholding South all is peace, quiet, plenty and contentment. We have no mobs, no trades unions, no strikes for higher wages, no armed resistance to the law, but little jealousy of the rich by the poor. We have but few in our jails, and fewer in our poor houses. We produce enough of the comforts and necessaries of life for a population three or four times as numerous as ours. We are wholly exempt from the torrent of pauperism, crime, agrarianism, and infidelity which Europe is pouring from her jails and alms houses on the already crowded North. Population increases slowly, wealth rapidly. In the tide water region of Eastern Virginia, as far as our experience extends, the crops have doubled in fifteen years, whilst the population has been almost stationary. In the same period the lands, owing to improvements of the soil and the many fine houses erected in the country, have nearly doubled in value. This ratio of improvement has been approximated or exceeded wherever in the South slaves are numerous. We have enough for the present, and no Malthusian spectres frightening us for the future. Wealth is more equally distributed than at the North, where a few millionaires own most of the property of the country. (These millionaires are men of cold hearts and weak minds; they know how to make money, but not how to use it, either for the benefit of themselves or of others.) High intellectual and moral attainments, refinement of head and heart, give standing to a man in the South, however poor he may be. Money is, with few exceptions, the only thing that ennobles at the North. We have poor among us, but none who are over-worked and under-fed. We do not crowd cities because lands are abundant and their owners kind, merciful and hospitable. The poor are as hospitable as the rich, the negro as the white man. Nobody dreams of turning a friend, a relative, or a stranger from his door. The very negro who deems it no crime to steal, would scorn to sell his hospitality. We have no loafers, because the poor relative or friend who borrows our horse, or spends a week under our roof, is a welcome guest. The loose economy, the wasteful mode of living at the South, is a blessing when rightly considered; it keeps want, scarcity and famine at a distance, because it leaves room for retrenchment. The nice, accurate economy of France, England and New England, keeps society always on the verge of famine, because it leaves no room to retrench, that is to live on a part only of what they now consume. Our society exhibits no appearance of precocity, no symptoms of decay. A long course of continuing improvement is in prospect before us, with no limits which human foresight can descry. Actual liberty and equality with our white population has been approached much nearer than in the free States. Few of our whites ever work as day laborers, none as cooks, scullions, ostlers, body servants, or in other menial capacities. One free citizen does not lord it over another; hence that feeling of independence and equality that distinguishes us; hence that pride of character, that self-respect, that gives us ascendancy when we come in contact with Northerners. It is a distinction to be a Southerner, as it was once to be a Roman citizen.

In Virginia we are about to reform our constitution. A fair opportunity will be afforded to draw a wider line of distinction between freemen and slaves, to elevate higher the condition of the citizen, to inspire every white man with pride of rank and position. We should do more for education. We have to educate but half of society, at the North they attempt to educate all. Besides, here all men have time for self-education, for reading and reflection. Nobody works long hours. We should prohibit the exercise of mechanic arts to slaves (except on their master's farm) and to free negroes. We should extend the right of suffrage to all native Virginians, and to Southerners who move to Virginia, over twenty-one years of age. We should permit no foreigner and no Northerner, who shall hereafter remove to the State, to vote in elections. We should have a small, well drilled, paid militia, to take the place of the patrol and the present useless militia system. All men of good character should serve on juries without regard to property qualification. Thus we should furnish honorable occupation to all our citizens, whilst we cultivated and improved their minds by requiring them all to take part in the administration of justice and of government. We should thus make poverty as honorable as it was in Greece and Rome; for to be a Virginian would be a higher distinction than wealth or title could bestow. We should cease to be a bye-word and reproach among nations for our love of the almighty dollar. We should be happy in the confidence that our posterity would never occupy the place of slaves, as half mankind must ever do in free society. Until the last fifteen years, our great error was to imitate Northern habits, customs and institutions. Our circumstances are so opposite to theirs, that whatever suits them is almost sure not to suit us. Until that time, in truth, we distrusted our social system. We thought slavery morally wrong, we thought it would not last, we thought it unprofitable. The Abolitionists assailed us; we looked more closely into our circumstances; became satisfied that slavery was morally right, that it would continue ever to exist, that it was as profitable as it was humane. This begat self-confidence, self-reliance. Since then our improvement has been rapid. Now we may safely say, that we are the happiest, most contented and prosperous people on earth. The inter-meddling of foreign pseudo-philanthopists in our affairs, though it has occasioned great irritation and indigna-tion, has been of inestimable advantage in teaching us to form a right estimate of our condition. This inter-meddling will soon cease; the poor at home in thunder tones demand their whole attention and all their charity. Self-preservation will compel them to listen to their de-mands. Moreover, light is breaking in upon us from abroad. All parties in England now agree that the attempt to put down the slave trade has greatly aggrava-ted its horrors, without at all diminishing the trade itself. It is proposed to withdraw her fleet from the African coast. France has already given notice that she will withdraw hers. America will follow the example. The emancipation of the slaves in the West Indies is ad-mitted to have been a failure in all respects. The late masters have been ruined, the liberated slaves refuse to work, and are fast returning to the savage state, and England herself has sustained a severe blow in the present diminution and prospective annihilation of the once enormous imports from her West Indian colonies.

In conclusion, we will repeat the propositions, in somewhat different phraseology, with which we set out. First—That Liberty and Equality, with their concomitant Free Competition, beget a war in society that is as destructive to its weaker members as the custom of exposing the deformed and crippled children. Secondly—That slavery protects the weaker members of society just as do the relations of parent, guardian and husband, and is as necessary, as natural, and almost as universal as those relations. Is our demonstration imperfect? Does universal experience sustain our theory? Should the conclusions to which we have arrived appear strange and startling, let them therefore not be rejected without examination. The world has had but little opportunity to contrast the working of Liberty and Equality with the old order of things, which always partook more or less of the character of domestic slavery. The strong prepossession in the public mind in favor of the new system, makes it reluctant to attribute the evil phenomena which it exhibits, to defects inherent in the system itself. That these defects should not have been foreseen and pointed out by any process of *a priori* reasoning, is but another proof of the fallibility of human sagacity and foresight when attempting to foretell the operation of new institutions. It is as much as human reason can do, when examining the complex frame of society, to trace effects back to their causes—much more than it can do, to foresee what effects new causes will produce. We invite investigation.

WHAT SHALL BE DONE

THE FREE NEGROES?

Nearly one half the civilized world is deeply interested in the solution of this question—but especially France, England and America. Already the emancipation of the blacks has occasioned many evils, and been productive of no ostensible good to themselves or to the whites. In the West Indian dominions of France and England, all industry is paralyzed, and the most fertile islands in the world threaten soon to become desert wastes, infested with lawless savages. The blacks so far outnumber the whites, that the latter will remove, or remain to witness the acting over again the tragedy of St. Domingo. The crusades occasioned less human suffering than has ensued or is certain to ensue from the emancipation of the blacks in the West Indies. The crusades, with all their iniquities, gave the first great impulse to civilization. West Indian emancipation has expelled civilization and veiled those lovely Isles with the thick curtain of ignorance and superstition. The masters have been robbed of their farms and of their slaves, with more millions than even Crœsus dreampt of—yet their loss is as nothing compared to the loss the slaves have sustained in being deprived of the tutelary guardianship of those masters. The masters may return to a civilized land—a land of law and order—there to enjoy the blessings of civilized life, perhaps to retrieve their ruined fortunes—or better still, to learn resignation to their fate at the altar of the Christian God. The emancipated negroes do not work, and hunger will soon drive them to every sort of crime. The light of Christianity, which was fast spreading amongst them, is destined to speedy extinction, and vile superstisions will supply its place. It is hardly too bold a figure to say that in losing his master, the negro has lost all hope here and hereafter. The civilized world has sustained a great loss in the diminution of the products of those Isles, which products have become the common food of half of mankind. But it is needless to enumerate the many evils that short-sighted philanthropy has inflicted on the West Indies and on the world at large, by emancipation, and equally needless to speculate about the remedy: there is no remedy, and it is not our business to propose it if there were.

In the United States the situation of the free blacks is becoming worse every day. The silly attempts of the Abolitionists to put them on a footing of equality with the whites, has exasperated the laboring whites at the North, and excited odium and suspicion against them at the South. The natural antipathies of race have been fanned into such a degree of excitement, that the free negro is bandied from pillar to post—from North to South and from South to North, till not a ray of hope is left him of a quiet, permanent residence any where, so long as he remains free. Illinois and California will not permit him to enter their dominions—

Ohio places him under severe conditions, and is now moving to expel him altogether, and Virginia also proposes to send him back to Africa. Mobs in our Northern cities drive him from his home and hunt him like a wild beast. Two great movements, or rather one great and one very small movement, may be observed in constant and busy operation as to the negro race. The small movement is that of the fanatical Abolitionists, who would free the whole race and put them on a social and political equality with the whites. The great movement is that proceeding from hostility of race, and proposes to get rid of the negroes altogether, not to free them. This movement is not confined to the North. Thousands, we regret to say, at the South, who think slavery a blessing to the negro, believe the negro a curse to the country. So far as the slaves are concerned, this opinion is fast changing. Men begin to look more closely at what the slaveholders have been doing since our Revolution, and find that they have been exceeded in skill, enterprise and industry, by no people under the sun. They have settled a vast territory from the Alleghany to the La Platte—from the Rio Grande to the Ohio, contending all the while with blood-thirsty savages and a climate more to be dreaded than even those savages themselves—and are already producing a greater agricultural surplus than any people in the world. They see, too, that the condition of the white man is elevated and equalized, for the blacks perform all menial duties and occupy the place of servants. The white laborers of the North think the existence of negroes at the North as free, or at the South as slaves,

injurious to themselves. They do not like the competition of human beings who have all the physical powers of men, with the wants only of brutes. Free Soil-
ism pretty well represents and embodies this feeling.
It is universal at the North, because the hostility to
negroes—the wish to get rid of their competition is universal there. It excludes free negroes from California
as well as slaves, showing that the Wilmot Proviso is
directed against the negro race—not against slavery.
This great movement, which proposes to get rid of negroes, rather than of slavery, is gathering strength every
day, and so far as the free negroes are concerned it
must soon sweep them away; for neither the feelings nor the interests of any part of the community,
except of a few crazy Abolitionists, can be enlisted in
their behalf. The slaves have masters to guard and
protect them—and guard, protect and *hold* them they
will, cost what it may.

The free negroes are no doubt an intolerable nuisance. They blight the prosperity of every village and
of every country neighborhood where they settle. They
are thieves from necessity, for nature has made them so
improvident they cannot in health provide for sickness,
in youth for old age, nor in summer for winter. Nature formed them for a climate where all their wants
were supplied abundantly by her liberal hand at every
season. We knew their natures when we set them free.
Should we blame them, or censure ourselves? We knew
they were not fitted for liberty, and yet conferred liberty on them. Our wiser ancestors made them slaves,
because as slaves they might be made civilized, useful

and christian beings. We subject children till twenty-one years of age to the control of their parents, or appoint guardians for them. We subject wives to the dominion of their husbands—apprentices to their masters. We permit sailors and soldiers to sell their liberties for terms of years. We send criminals to jails and penitentiaries, and lunatics to hospitals. In all these cases, we take away the liberties of the whites, either for the benefit of individuals or for the good of society. We act upon the principle that no one is entitled to liberty who will abuse it to the detriment of himself or of others. The *law* curtails and restricts the freedom of the wisest and the best;—the *straight jacket* and *manacles* of iron are applied to the weakest and most wicked. There is no perfect liberty with the whites, but every degree of slavery, from law to straight jackets. The free blacks, who most need the control of masters, guardians, curators or committees are left to the enjoyment of the largest liberty. *Law* alone is expected to control and regulate their conduct. We had as well publish laws to our herds and flocks. Men, to be governed by mere law, must possess great intelligence, and have acquired habits of self-control and self-denial. The whites from 15 to 21 years of age lack not intelligence, but habits of self-control, to fit them for government by law alone. The arbitrary will of the parent or guardian must be superadded to the mandates of the law, to save them from the indiscretions into which their feelings and their passions would lead them. The free negroes as a class, have less intelligence and less self-control, than the whites over 15

years of age. A good government graduates as nicely
as is practicable. each man's liberty to his capacity for
its enjoyment—it is obliged, however, to establish general rules, and thus occasions many cases of individual hardship. The white male adults, over twenty-one
years of age, are presumed to possess enough of virtue,
intelligence and self-control, to be left with no other
control than that of the law—yet of those we meet
with thousands who from habitual drunkenness, from
excessive improvidence and extravagance, or from strong
criminal propensities, are wholly unfitted for the government of mere law, and stand in need of the will of
a superior to control their conduct, and save them from
ruining themselves, their friends and families. On the
other hand, we find many instances of wisdom and prudence among whites under 21 years of age, whom the
law, nevertheless, subjects to the control of guardians
and parents often less wise, less virtuous, and less prudent than themselves. In subjecting the free blacks
to the will of white masters, fewer instances of injustice
of this kind would occur, than now occur with the
whites, because as a class they are less fitted for self-
government than the whites between the ages of 15
and 21. A free negro! Why, the very term seems
an absurdity. It is our daily boast, and experience veri-
fies it, that the Anglo-Saxons of America are the only
people in the world fitted for freedon. The negro's is
not human freedom, but the wild and vicious license of
the fox, the wolf or the hawk. He is, from the necessity of his nature, a very Ishmaelite, whose hand is
against every man, and every man's hand is against

him. It is as much the duty of government to take away liberty from those who abuse it, as to confer it on those who use it properly. It practises every day, as we have shewn, on this principle, in its treatment of the whites, and why should it hesitate to do so in regard to the blacks? It is the object and duty of government to protect men, not merely from wrong and injustice from others, but from the consequences of their own vices, imprudence and improvidence. The humblest member of society, no matter what the color of his skin, has a right to this protection. The experience of all ages, and of all countries, shows that this protection to a weaker race like the negro, living among a superior race, can only be given by bestowing on him a master whose will shall be the law of his conduct, whose skill and foresight shall amass and provide for him in sickness and in old age, and whose power shall shield him from the consequences of his own improvidence. The vassalage and serfdom of Europe, the slavery of America, and the peonage of Mexico, alike point to this as the natural and proper method of governing free negroes. The wisdom of the common law, and indeed of all ancient codes, distinctly teaches the same truth; for guardians, parents, husbands, committees, and various officers, are but masters by another name. They are all intended to supply, in more or less degree, that want of self-control which unfits large classes of the whites for self-government. But there is a peculiar necessity for some measure of this kind, with regard to the blacks, growing out of the antipathies of race. They are threatened with violent extermination.

M

The fate of the Indians shows that they will be exterminated, if they continue so useless and so troublesome. Had the Indian been useful as a slave, he would have survived and become a civilized and christian being; but he was found as useless, as troublesome, and as intractable as a beast of prey, and has shared the fate of a beast of prey. The negro, in the condition of slavery, is a happy, contented, and useful being. It is the state for which nature intended, and to which our ancestors, quite as wise and virtuous as ourselves, consigned him. We have fully and fairly tried the experiment of freeing him; we have witnessed its universal and deplorable failure, and it is now our right and our duty, to listen to the voice of wisdom and experience, and re-consign him to the only condition for which he is suited.

There is another and an urgent reason why his very existence requires that he should be subjected to some modification of slavery. His lot is cast among the Anglo-Saxon race, and what people can stand free competition with that race? The Romans conquered England, and the ancient Britons flourished and became civilized under their rule. The Saxon, Dane and Norman came, and nothing remains to tell of the existence of the Britons but the names of a few rivers. The Indian is exterminated from Maine to Georgia, the Hindoos are perishing under British rule by millions, the Spaniard is hardly heard of in Florida, and Peonage alone can save the Mexican from annihilation. From the days of Hengist and Horsa, to those of Houston, the same adventurous, rapacious, exterminating spirit has characterised the race. Can the negro live with all his reckless improvidence under the shade of this Upas tree, whose deadly poison spares no other race? Is he fitted to compete with a people who, in the struggle of life, have outstripped and exterminated all other nations with whom they have come in contact? No. Throwing out of view the signs of the times, pregnant with growing hate and hostility to the free negro, the experience of the past shows that his present condition is hopeless; but make him property, and this same Anglo-Saxon will protect, guard and cherish him, for no people on earth love property more, will go greater lengths, so far as danger is concerned, to obtain it, or take better care of it after it is obtained.

We will not undertake to decide what degree or modification of servitude shall be adopted, but will suggest that peonage, which is probably one of its mildest forms, might be instituted. To attain this, it is only necessary to repeal so much of the common law as prevents a man's parting with his personal liberty. Indeed, the common law, in the cases of soldiers and sailors, permits even white men to sell themselves and bind their persons for a term of years. Grant the same privilege to the free negro at all times, and we think there will be few of them left free in ten years to come. They cannot now, we know from experience, obtain much more than half the yearly hire of slaves, because the hirer has no security that they will remain till the end of the year. Their improvidence, and their desire to obtain the protection of some white man, would drive them all into contracts of this kind. The nuisance would thus be abated, and in its place we should acquire a class of strong, healthy laborers. If this plan did not work well, the State authorities should, at the beginning of each year, hire all those out who owned not enough property to support themselves. Part of the hires might be paid over to them, and the balance retained as a fund to support the infants, the aged, and infirm here, or used as a means to send them all to Africa. If experience showed that nothing short of absolute slavery would meet the exigencies of the case, then give them a year's notice to quit the State, or be sold into unconditional slavery. This last alternative would still place them in a situation of much greater security and comfort than they now any where enjoy, or can ever probably enjoy, in a state of unlimited freedom. We think it a more humane measure, and a more politic one, than to send them to Africa. If it be necessary, it must be right. Reducing men to slavery has been practised throughout all time, and by men as good, and as wise as ourselves. Practised too, continually, upon men much better, much wiser, and much more suited for freedom than the negro. There is more of selfishness, less of exalted, chivalrous disinterested virtue in this utilitarian age, than in most of those with which we are acquainted, that have preceded it. We only

> Compound for sins *we* are inclined to,
> By damning those *we* have no mind to.

Liberty is the great hobby of this money-making age, and the over-ruling argument in its favor is borrowed from the arithmetic. "Free labor is more productive than slave labor. It is cheaper to hire the laborer, when you want him, and turn him out to starve when you have done with him, than to buy a slave and support him through all the seasons of the year, and through all the periods of his life. Besides, the free man whose very life depends on it, will work harder than the slave, who is sure of a support, whether he works or not." Since the slave-trade is abolished, which was a lucrative and favorite pursuit of the Yankees and English, those gentry have, from the above interested calculations, turned abolitionists. Our Southern patriots, at the time of the Revolution, finding negroes expensive and useless, became warm anti-slavery men. We, their wiser sons, having learned to make cotton and sugar, find slavery very useful and profitable, and think it a most excellent institution. We of the South advocate slavery, no doubt, from just as selfish motives as induce the Yankees and English to deprecate it. We have, however, almost all human and divine authority on our side of the argument. The Bible no where condemns, and throughout recognises slavery. Slavery has been so universal in the civilized world, and so little, if at all known among savages, that its occasional absence of late years in civilized nations, seems to indicate something wrong or rotten in their condition. The starving state of the poor in all such countries, furnishes the solution of the difficulty, and indicates the character of the disease under which society is suffering. They have become too poor to have slaves, whom the law would oblige them to support. We have never met with a Southern man, *of late years*, who did not think slavery a blessing to the negro race. We have never heard a single white man maintain that this race was qualified for freedom, nor met with one who did not complain of the free negroes as a nuisance. Now, how strange and inconsistent in us to permit men to remain free, whose freedom is a curse to themselves and a nuisance to society. How cruel and unwise in us not to extend the blessings of slavery to the free negroes, which work so well with the slaves. Humanity, self-interest, consistency, all require that we should enslave the free negro. We enslave the whites whenever the good of the individual, or of society requires it, in the many instances we have cited, and leave the free negro to roam at large in liberty as untrammelled and unconstrained as that of the beasts of the field or birds of the air. They are restrained neither by the conventionalities of society, the bonds of religion, the laws of morality, the chain of marriage, the authority of parents or guardians, nor by the power of a master. They who are least fitted for liberty are scarcely subjected to any governmental control whatever.

But if *they* be qualified for liberty, so are our slaves, and we are acting morally wrong in retaining in bondage beings who would be better off as freemen. The slave, if set free, would be just what the free negroes now are, and if that be a desirable condition, one better for them and for society, than that they are now in, we ought to set about making free negroes of them. Both cases are before us, we have ample experience of the working of both. It is not only our right, but our duty to cherish and encourage that condition of the negro race which works well—to abolish that which works badly.

The free negroes corrupt our slaves and make them less contented with their situation. Their competition is injurious to our white laboring citizens. Their wants are so few and simple, that when they do work, they will take lower wages than the white man can afford to receive; besides, it is as well the policy as the duty of the State to elevate the condition of her citizens, not to send them in the labor market with negroes for competitors. Let the negro always occupy a situation subordinate to the white man. North and South, every deviation from this policy leads to violence, in which the blacks are the sufferers. The law cannot make negroes free if it would, because society will not tolerate it. The signs of the times, North and South, clearly show that the free negroes will be borne with no longer by society. If the subject be promptly attended to by State governments, some disposition of them may be made consistent with humanity. If legislative action be delayed, the people in their primary capacity, in vulgar parlance mobs, will take the case in hand. We heard but recently, that the people in one of our counties had given them notice to quit. Quit! and go where? To be turned out and hunted like the bagged fox.

II.

Is there any good reason why men should not be allowed to sell their liberty? Is it wise, politic or humane, to prevent the man, who sees his family starving around him, from hiring himself so as to bind his person, even for a day, a week, or a month, to save himself and family from death? Could the poor Irish sell themselves and families for a term of years, to the farmers of our Northwestern States, in order to pay their passage to this country, and secure them from want on their arrival, would there be any thing unwise or unmerciful in the laws which permitted it? The law did once permit it, for Virginia was in great part settled by indented servants, and by the descendants of girls bought up in London and sold to the planters here for wives. Indeed, all women literally sell their liberties when they marry, and very few repent of the bargain. Among the civilized States of antiquity, the right to sell one's liberty, we believe, was universal. Is it not a curtailment of liberty to deny the right? The starving poor would often think so. To the victim of intemperance who has just recovered from an attack of delirium tremens, such a right would be worth all the temperance societies in the world. His enervated will can no longer control him, and the law will not permit him to adopt the will of another. The law thus murders thousands annually, pretending all the while to guard and protect their rights. The army, the navy and the merchant service are filled with men of this description. It is the only refuge the law allows them. Those who were fitted for liberty would not sell it, or if in some moment of misfortune they did, they would buy that liberty again by the exercise of great economy and industry. The right to purchase their own liberty has, in other countries, been a common privilege of slaves. We mean that white men sold into slavery would, if worthy of liberty, purchase their freedom. We do not advocate any change of the law that would permit them to part, even for a day, with their personal liberty. One of the objects in granting such privilege to free negroes, would be to draw a wider line of distinction between the negroes and our white citizens. But in countries where there are no negroes, we can see no reason why the whites in all cases might not be allowed to sell their persons for short periods. Soldiers and sailors are allowed to do so for the defence of the nation and the benefit of commerce. Domestic servants and farm hands would be benefited themselves, and their employers also benefited, could they be hired by the year; at all events, every government that denies this privilege of selling one's self, is bound to provide for its poor citizens, as well as masters provide for their slaves. But all governments permit thousands of the poor to starve—in truth, every body seems to have taken it for granted that this provision of the law is right, without having taken the trouble to examine into the reasons on which it is founded. The reasons assigned by Blackstone in his Commentaries, are so false and puerile, as to show that he had given no consideration to the subject. The objection that a man may not sell himself, because slavery puts his life in his master's hands, is false as to modern slavery in all civilized countries, and 'tis with this slavery we and he too had to deal. The other objection, that the slave's property belongs to the master, is not a necessary or universal feature of slavery. We would not have it so in the case of the free negroes, when placed, as we hope they will be, in some modified condition of slavery. His third objection, that the consideration accrues to the master, is only true when the slave can hold no separate property. In most cases, no consideration would be paid, other than protection and support. Justice will compel us, in some cases, to pay hire for the free negroes, but we know from experience that morality forbids it. We hire a free negro by the year—we feed and clothe him, and he is anxious to continue with us another year. We know that he spends almost every cent of his hire in vice and debauchery, yet he is superior to his race generally, for he is honest and industrious. We pay him a third less hire than we would give for him had he the right to bind his person. Free negroes generally hire for little more than half what slaves do: liberty costs them dear. Whilst on this subject, we would call attention to a new kind of African slave-trade that prevails in our neighborhood; the free negro women hire out their children, and bask in the sun idle and unemployed themselves. We tried to persuade, some days since, a young negro man, who, with his young wife, were desperately poor, that he would be better off as a slave, as he might expect soon to have a large family to support, and could now scarce support himself. He quaintly replied, "that he then would hire out his children and live easy."

Blackstone, treating of the relative position of master an￼ ￼ ￼ m lo s t followin language: "The first sort of servants, therefore, acknowledged by the laws of England, are *menial servants,* so called from being *intra moenia,* or domestics. The contract between them and their masters arises upon the hiring. If the hiring be general, without any particular time limited, the law considers it to be a hiring for a year, upon a principle of natural equity that the servant shall serve and the master maintain him throughout all the revolutions of the respective seasons, as well when there is work to be done as when there is not—but the contract may be made for any longer or smaller term. All single men, between twelve years old and sixty, and married ones under thirty years of age—and all single women between twelve and forty, not having any visible livelihood, are compellable by two justices to go out to service in husbandry or other specific trades for the promotion of honest industry, and no master can put away his servant, or servant leave his master, after being so retained, either before or at the end of his term, without a quarter's warning; unless upon reasonable cause, to be allowed by a justice of the peace; but they may part by consent, or make a special bargain."

Now, a statute in our State, with regard to free negroes which should attain the ends contemplated by this English statute, would rid us of the nuisance. To attain those ends, the contract of hiring should be for a year or longer period, and should bind the person.

The Roman history contains a remarkable proof of the kindly and friendly relations which subordination of rank begets. The Plebeians all became the clients or vassals of some Patrician, who was bound to advise, counsel and protect them. In all the vicissitudes of the Republic, during a lapse of six hundred years, we are told that not a single instance occurred of faithlessness to this tie of inferior and superior. The attachment between client and patron descended from father to son, and made one family of the protector and protected. How much more does the free negro need a patron than did the Roman. Curious speculators on society, seeing that hereditary distinctions of rank gradually disappear in nations, have concluded that these distinctions were all induced by conquest and difference of race. No length of time will wear out the distinction between blacks and whites; but proper subordination of the black to the white man will be sure to produce the usual attachment between lord and vassal, master and slave, protector and protected. The fate of the Gipsey race in England shows the impossibility of governing half-civilized beings by mere law. The laws against them were numerous and bloody, and influenced their conduct no more than laws passed against crows and blackbirds. They heeded not the precepts and admonitions of the law, and have been exterminated by the avenging sword of the law. Such has been the fate of the Indians, and such will be the fate of the free negroes, if mobs, to the eternal disgrace of our country, do not anticipate the law. History furnishes but a single instance where negroes have been well governed without masters, and in that instance the rule was ten times more rigorous than that of the master. Tousaint, the president of Hayti, by a strict military surveillance, kept them at work on separate farms, and punished them capitally for the third offence of quitting the farm without a written permit. Succeeding administrations have relaxed the government till the whole island is in a state of savage anarchy which invites and would justify another conquest and reduction of the inhabitants to that state of slavery for which alone they are fitted, and from which they so wickedly escaped.

The great mortality, the vice and ignorance that prevail at the British colony of Sierra Leone, show that this attempt to improve the condition of the negro has resulted in consequences infinitely worse than slavery. Better governments at Liberia and Cape Palmas have prevented, so far, the exhibition of so much gross vice and ignorance; but even in those colonies the mortality is so great as to deter those who value human life as the greatest of human blessings from encouraging emigration to them. But if almost certain death from the climate did not await the emigrant negroes, they must be extirpated by the savages, or extirpate the savages to make room for themselves. No habitable part of Africa is unsettled, and the free blacks who go there in numbers must make room for themselves, sword in hand, as the whites did in America. We who maintain that it was a blessing to the negro to be brought from Africa and made a slave and a Christian, are estopped from contending that it is also a blessing to set him free and send him back to become a savage and a Pagan. Between the two blessings, the middle passage on the inward trip and the climate of the coast on the return, few would survive to tell of their happiness.

Let us try the experiment of hiring them by the year, and if that fail, sell them into unconditional slavery.

Slavery is a blessing to the negro—at all events, it is better than the tender mercies of an American mob or an African cannibal, the Scylla and Charybdis which now threaten him. Slavery is too costly, too humane and merciful an institution for France, England or New England. The free competition of labor and capital in those countries where labor is redundant, is certain to bring the wages of labor down to the minimum amount that will support human life. The employers of free laborers, like the riders of hired horses, try to get the most possible work out of them, for the least hire. They boast of the low rates at which they procure labor, and still hold up their heads in society uncensured and unreproved. No slaveholder was ever so brutal as to boast of the low wages he paid his slaves, to pride himself on feeding and clothing them badly—neglecting the young, the aged, the sick and infirm; such a man would be hooted from society as a monster. Society hardly tolerates inhumanity to horses, much less to slaves. But disguise the process a little, and it is a popular virtue to oppress free white poor people. Get the labor of the able-bodied husband as cheap as you can, and leave his wife, children and aged parents to starve, and you are the beau ideal of a man in England and New England. Public opinion, as well as natural feeling, requires a man to pay his slave high wages; the same public opinion commends your cleverness in paying low wages to free laborers, and nature and conscience oppose no obstacles to the screwing process.

> KING LEAR.— ——— Take physic, pomp;
> Expose thyself to feel what wretches feel,
> That thou mayest shake the superflux to them,
> And show the heavens more just.

III.

To say that free labor is cheaper than slave labor, is to say that the slave is better off, so far as physical comfort is concerned, than the free laborer. The wages of the free laborer exactly represent all the physical material comforts he and his family can · enjoy—the cost of slave labor consists (after the slaves are purchased) entirely of the comforts of life which the master gives to his slaves. The hirer of free laborers maintains the families of those laborers, in sickness and in health, in infancy and in old age, precisely as does the master his slaves—the only difference being that the free laborer expends the hire himself for those purposes, whilst the master expends it for the slave. If free labor be cheapest, it is because it costs the employer less to support the free laborer and his family, than it does the master to support his slaves. Price is the measure of things useful to man. If the slave's labor costs more than the free man's, he gets a larger measure of things useful to mankind. Now this is exact or demonstrative reasoning, because it treats of quantities of things physical or material, which admit of admeasurement. Mathematical certainty is attainable by argument of this kind. We think, (granting our premises, that free labor is cheaper than slave labor,) we have attained this degree of certainty. We add as a corollary, that the slave's physical condition is exactly so much better than the free laborer's, as the cost of slave labor exceeds that of free labor. Now, as to the relative moral condition of the slave and the free laborer, reasoning of this kind cannot be employed at all, because we have to deal with things moral and metaphysical, in which there are no ascertainable quantities—no standard of admeasurement to appeal to. We can measure the physical comforts of life—such as food, raiment, &c., in various ways; but all of them, by the common, agreed standard of price—the amount of dollars and cents which they cost—but we cannot measure morality, virtue, hope, happiness, despair, &c. To illustrate, the slave feels secure for himself and family, of future comfortable maintenance, but hopeless as to bettering his condition. The free laborer is harrowed with fears and apprehensions of the future, but along with these fears and apprehensions, entertains the hope of changing and improving his condition. In these cases we can get at no precise quantities—appeal to no standard of measure, to determine whether the attributes of slavery, or those of liberty are of greater quantity or value. We launch on a sea of moral or speculative reasoning, where we cannot approximate any thing like proof—each man's taste will be the only arbiter, and de gustibus non est disputandum. We have inverted, intentionally, the correct order of reasoning. We come in the last place to prove our premises; we knew the reader would admit them till he saw the conclusions to which they infallibly led—then many a reader will revolt at those premises, because they lead to what are, in his mind, revolting conclusions. First, then, free labor is cheaper than slave labor, in a thickly settled country, else the European nations who sent slaves to America would have also employed them at home; for it is notorious that as a general, almost an universal rule, farmers and other capitalists employ that labor which is cheapest.

Secondly. The slave-holding South is supplied by the North and other non-slaveholding countries, with all articles that can be made as well at the North as at the South—which proves that it is cheaper to employ free labor to make those articles and pay the expenses of transportation, than to have them made by slaves at home.

Thirdly. In all old countries there is a superfluity of laborers, and they, in competing to get employment, under-bid each other, till wages reach the lowest point, that will support human existence; but the master is afraid so to depress the wages of his slave, else he might lose the slave.

Fourthly. The Puritan fathers and their immediate descendants were active slave-traders and slave-holders— their later posterity, neither more pious nor moral than their ancestors or their Southern neighbors, liberated their slaves, we may fairly infer, because they found free labor cheaper.

Fifthly. It has been generally admitted by the opponents of slavery that free labor is cheaper.

Having demonstrated that the physical condition of the slave is better than that of the free laborer, it remains only that we should apply this conclusion to the free negroes whom we propose to enslave. Their physical condition would be improved by slavery, and their moral condition could not be made worse, for, unlike the white man, they have no hope of changing and

improving their condition whilst free. They canno
escape from the class of common laborers. The white
above them oppose an insuperable barrier to their ele
vation. It is certainly better to be a slave than a fre
laborer, without hope of improving one's condition.

[NOTE.—We have left out the original cost of th
slaves, in estimating the relative cheapness of slav
and free, because formerly African slaves cost so littl
as not to have seriously influenced the preference give
to free labor in Europe, and more recently our Norther
States, after incurring that cost, found it cheaper t
liberate the slaves and employ free labor.]

IV.

Has the State the right to enslave them? / Slaver
is but a form of government, and we have shewn it i
the duty and practice of every State to adopt the de
gree of control and form of government as near a
practicable to the capacity and necessity of each indi
vidual. Guardians are provided for children, master
for apprentices, captains for sailors and soldiers, dar
cells and hard work for convicts, and straight jacket
for lunatics. No one doubts that it is as well the righ
as the duty of government to make these provisions
and abridge or take away liberty from all white citizen
who are not qualified to enjoy it. Every other for
of government than that of slavery has signally faile
in the case of the negro. He is an enemy to himself,
and an intolerable pest and nuisance to society, where
ever among the whites he is free. The Abolitionists

ceeded wonderfully in aggravating and embittering the natural hostility of the white and black race. They have prompted the free negroes to assert their equality with the whites, and in return for their insolence, the whites are ready to expel them from the land. But expulsion is now, at least, impracticable. If it ever succeeds, it will require ages to complete it. In the meantime, it is the right and duty of the State to enslave them, because experience has clearly proved that it is the only practicable mode of governing them. We deprive them of no right, because no one, black or white, has a right to liberty who abuses it to the detriment of himself or of society. They have the right to the protection and care of masters, but the law denies them the exercise of that right in not permitting them to hire or sell themselves. The common notion that liberty is good for man, is one of the most false and foolish that ever entered the human mind. None but brutes and savages desire entire liberty. The only free people in the world are the Digger Indians of the Valley of the Great Salt Lake and the Australians of New Holland; they know nothing of government, of society, of castes, of classes, or of subordination of rank; each man digs for worms and climbs for birds' eggs on his own hook; they are perfectly free, famished and degraded. We admire and love liberty, coupled with happiness, as much as any one. We pine with the caged bird, and rejoice with the free warblers of the grove and the forest. The sportive gambols of the colt fill us with pleasure.

Quæ velut latis equa trima campis
Ludit exultim metuit que tangi.

Nature has fitted such creatures for liberty; but of cold, shivering, naked, houseless, starving liberty, the liberty of the prodigal son and the free negro, we entertain much the same opinion that Falstaff did of honor:—"What is honor? A word. What is in that word honor? What is that honor? Air. A trim reckoning!—Who hath it? He who died o' Wednesday. Doth he feel it? No. Doth he hear it? No. Is it insensible then? Yea, to the dead. But it will not live with the living—therefore I'll none of it. Honor is a mere scutcheon, and so ends my catechism." As civilization advances liberty recedes. The Cossacks of Russia are a thousand times more free than the enlightened inhabitants of the city of New York. The Cossacks, living far from government, and having little property, are scarcely aware that a government exists. The enlightened citizen of New York daily feels the operation of the laws of the Union, the laws of the State, and the laws of the corporation; he is probably a member of a church, a club, of a Masonic society, and of a board of trade—he is controlled in his conduct by the rules, regulations and laws of all these institutions; besides, he is the slave of fashion, and cannot, like the savage, dress and appear as he pleases: he has a wife and children to attend to and provide for, and all his spare moments must be devoted to them. Does such a man enjoy one moment of liberty? No; every moment has its appropriate duties, which he must slavishly perform, or he is a disgraced man. It is true, his slavery is self-imposed in a great measure. This only shews that civilized man does not desire liberty. Was there ever a white savage—we mean one of the Caucasian race—except the wild Boy of Hanover? The Greeks and Romans were very lavish of the term barbarian, but we doubt whether they ever saw a savage. Herodotus treats of men without heads and with eyes in their breasts, in Africa, but says not a word of men with black skins and woolly heads. His learning, which embraces on this subject all known by his countrymen, only extended to the limits of civilization. Have the whites been civilized in some degree from the days of Noah, or did civilization in the middle ages spread with electric speed through Norway, Sweden, Lapland and Russia? It matters not which proposition be true. The white race has either been always civilized, or has evinced a remarkable aptitude to adopt civilization; they required no missionaries and colonization societies to civilize them.

Alexander Everett, a Northern gentleman, in a work on America, contends that civilization had its birth with the negroes, and that the rest of the world derived it from them. In locating the birth-place of civilization, he very nearly concurs with a majority of the learned. The records of history and the remains of art alike designate the banks of the lower Nile as the cradle of civilization. For four thousand years, certainly, the negro race has been in immediate contact with civilization. A dense population, without interruption or interval, for ages before the time of Pharaoh and Moses, extended along the Nile from the Pyramids and Thebais to the negroes along the white Nile. Between Thebais and the negroes, an interval of a few hundred miles was settled by people of Arabic descent—a people from the days of Abraham always more or less civilized. Yet with all the advantage of contact with civilization for four thousand years, not a single negro was ever reclaimed from his savage state till he was caught, tied, tamed and domesticated like the wild ox or the wild horse. Talk of sending missionaries to such a people! Why, millions of missionaries have been side by side with them for four thousand years, and none but the slave-dealer ever made a convert. War, pestilence and famine are the best missionaries to teach civilization, (except the conjunction of a thin skin and a hard frost,) for necessity is the mother of invention, civilization but accumulated invention, and war, pestilence and famine the great necessities which prompt men to invent, and teach them to remember and improve what they invent. A people so imbecile in intellect, or so improvident as not to be civilized by these great necessities, can only be civilized by slavery. The horse and ox will not willingly submit to the yoke to provide for the exigencies of winter, however eloquently you discourse to them on the necessity and propriety of such conduct; no more will the negro. A crazy poet or an Irish orator (in love with universal emancipation,) would permit the horse and the negro to luxuriate in liberty in the summer and starve in winter. Not so a sensible Englishman and profound philosopher like Carlyle, to whom we are indebted for this illustration. He thinks the liberated negroes in the West Indies are no more operated on in the regulation of their lives, by reason, than the horse or the ox. But like the ox and ass, the negro may be domesticated; he is not like the Indian of America, an animal *feræ naturæ*. The Indian, like the savage races of Canaan, is doomed to extermination, and those who most sympathize with his fate would be the first to shoot him if they lived on the frontier. God did not direct his chosen people to exterminate all races; such as were fit for slaves they were ordered to make slaves of. Despite the mawkish sensibility of the age, practical men are, without the aid of immediate revelation, pursuing the same course; they slay the Indians hip and thigh, as in the days of Moses and Joshua, and enslave the negroes. "There is nothing new under the sun." This is all right, because it is necessary. Father Bacchus (when drunk, no doubt,) and the last exhibitor of wild beasts in New York, (*Quid non mortalia pectora cogis, auri sacra fames,*) drove lions to their cars; yet lions to-day are as useless and ferocious as in the days of Bacchus; and the Indian of to-day is as fierce and wild as those who met Columbus on the beach.

> " Like the fox,
> Who, ever so tame, so cherished and locked up,
> Will have a wild trick of his ancestors."

In his proper sphere, we love and respect the negro. He is eminently docile, imitative and parasitical. He will not go to Liberia, nor to the West Indies, because he has too much good sense to trust his fate to a community of negroes. He knows he is the ivy, and would cling to the white oak, not to the ivy, for support. He respects, as we do, some of the Abolitionists, because many of them are men who will make any sacrifice of their time and money to achieve what they think right. They are crazy Quixotes, no doubt, but their high aims and lofty disinterestedness make them far more respectable than they would be as plain, plodding farmers of La Mancha. Don Quixote mad, is the noblest, because the most chivalrous and disinterested of all the heroes of Epic poetry; he is but a drivelling, penitent dotard when he recovers. We would as soon stop a crusader or a fox-hunter in mid career, and prove to him the folly of his pursuit, as cure these Abolitionists of their madness. Such illusions afford so much higher pleasure than the sober realities of life, that it is the part of true philosophy to cherish, not dispel them. Much the larger portion of the abolitionists are, however, men of very different characters—Catilines and Jack Cades, men of desperate fortunes and desperate morals, who make as fierce war on landed property at home as they do on slavery abroad. The negroes despise the Clay clique of Colonizationists, because, believing slavery morally wrong, they have not the courage to say so, nor the justice to give the slave up. If slavery be wrong, the abolitionists are right. We say to the colonizationists, you cannot send the free negroes away. They have felt the coming storm, they have intermarried with the slaves, they have hired themselves to the farmers, and cling and cluster about the penates at the very horns of the domestic altar.

> Hic Hecuba, et natæ necquiquam altaria circum
> Precipites atra, ceu tempestate Columbæ
> Condensæ, et Divum amplexæ semulacra tenebant.

No ruthless Pyrrhus shall tear them thence. They are the guests of the farmer, and the Turk holds not hospitality half so sacred as the Southern farmer. His house is his castle, which he will defend to the last extremity against all intrusion. The barons of Runimede have their exact prototype in the Southern farmer. Better beard the lion in his den than touch any thing that has entered the sacred precinct of his farm.

But the free negro is not only the guest; he is, for the time, the property of the farmer; and Shakspeare has well expressed the English sense of property, from the lips of an Italian speaking of his wife :

> PETRUCHIO.—I will be master of what is my own ;
> She is my goods, my chattels ; she is my house,
> My household stuff, my field, my barn,
> My horse, my ox, my ass, my any thing,
> And here she stands ; touch her whoever dare.

Thus will the farmer defend the free negro who has selected him for his patron and master. Whilst on the subject of Shakspeare, we would invite those who think that slavery degrades the character of the slave, to read the play of " As you like it." They will find old Adam a more elevated character than any anti-slavery man that ever lived—and the character is true to nature.

> "ADAM.—Master, go on, and I will follow thee
> To the last gasp, with truth and loyalty."

Equality begets universal envy, meanness and uncharitableness—slavery elevates and purifies the sentiments of master and slave.

To return from this digression—very many of the free negroes, alarmed by the portentous signs of the times, threatening them with extermination or expulsion, have attached themselves to white masters. Will our legis-

N

lators sanction and encourage these contracts, or will they send them all to Africa? Suppose the project succeeds, and all the free negroes are shipped off—how long will it be before we are called to send off our slaves also?

Northern abolition quieted and the free negroes sent off, may not gradual emancipation rear its head and prove a worse enemy, because a domestic one, than any with which we have had to contend? But a small portion of the Southern press even now undertakes to justify slavery, to maintain that it is right in the abstract, morally right; that it is expedient or profitable. Will not this press, when foreign interference is quieted, and the free negroes removed, become the advocate of gradual emancipation? As they say not a word to justify slavery, we presume they think it wrong; and if so, it is their duty, as conscientious men, to embrace the first safe occasion to get rid of it.

The Abolitionists themselves furnish the most conclusive evidence that slavery must exist in every society until human nature itself is changed. Nay, they propose to change all man's nature, in order to fit him for that social equality, that community of property, and of other things more sacred than property, which they would erect on the ruins of our present system of society. The Ohio ladies hate slavery, and seeing that marriage brings about one of the forms of slavery, to be consistent, they will have no more marriages after the old fashion. Separate property, too, gives power to those who hold property to command the labor of those who hold none. "Property," say they, "is a thief!" and must be abolished. The Bible commands wives to obey their husbands, and slaves their masters; the Bible must be cast into the flames! Christianity and Socialism are deadly enemies. But after all the institutions of society are destroyed, families abolished, churches demolished, the Bible burnt, and property held in common, still they have the candor to admit that the selfishness of human nature would for a time disturb the harmonious working of their system. They promise us, however, that a few generations would change and perfect man's nature, and then Socialism would work admirably. At the end of the time we suspect they would become converts to the sage reflection of Christopher North : "There is a great deal of human nature in man !" We treat the Abolitionists and Socialists as identical, because they are notoriously the same people, employing the same arguments and bent on the same schemes. Abolition is the first step in Socialism; the former proposes to abolish negro slavery, the latter all kinds of slavery—religion, government, marriage, families, property—nay, human nature itself. Yet the former contains the germ of the latter, and very soon ripens into it; Abolition is Socialism in its infancy. Ladies of Ohio ! Horace Greely ! Socialists of France ! Is it not so ?

SLAVERY JUSTIFIED.

THE SUBJECT CONTINUED.

Alton Locke, Tailor and Poet: an Auto-biography: has recently been the subject of review in the Edinburgh, the North British, and Blackwood. Each of these able Reviews admits that Alton Locke, in the main, gives a fair picture of the state of the poor in England, and that their condition is intolerable, and daily growing worse. Blackwood and the North British Review farther admit, with the Socialists, that this desperate condition of the poor is owing to free competition, or liberty; and even the Edinburgh, with all its love for political economy, distinctly alleges that a cure for the sufferings of the working classes may be found by recurring to the old order of things :—feudalism, vassalage and serfdom. It further appears from these Reviews, that socialism, with thinking men, is almost universal in England. Except the Edinburgh Review, and a little clique that adhere to it, all men agree that free competition has brought on the evils under which the Empire is suffering, and that free competition must be checked and corrected, or the Empire be subverted. Now free competition is nothing in the world but the absence of domestic slavery, and these Reviews, all though afraid to use the word, do in effect distinctly admit that the intolerable condition of the working classes is owing to the absence of that form of domestic slavery which afforded support and protection to the poor in feudal times. Experience has universally shown, that the slavery of the working classes to the rich, which grows out of liberty and equality, or free competition, is ten times more onerous and exacting than domestic slavery. The bathos of human misery is to be a slave without a master. Such is the condition of the poor in the free States of Europe; they are slaves without masters. They have no houses, no property, none to protect them, none to care for them. In the fierce competition for employment, the intense struggle to get a livelihood, and the ruinous underbidding it occasions, we see the rich devouring the poor, and the poor devouring one another. This process is well described by the Chartist, Crossthwaite, in Alton Locke:

"It is a sin to add our weight to the crowd of artisans who are now choking and strangling each other to death, as the prisoners did in the black hole of Calcutta. Let those who will, turn beasts of prey and feed upon their fellows; but let us at least keep ourselves pure. It may be the law of political civilization, that the rich should eat up the poor, and the poor eat up each other. Then, I here rise and curse that law, that civilization, that nature. Either I will destroy them or they shall destroy me. As a slave, as an increased burden on my fellow-sufferers, I will not live. So help me God! I will take no more work to my house, and I call upon all to sign a protest to that effect."

England is a Garden of Eden, in which the birds of the air, the fishes of the sea, and the beasts of the field participate equally with the owners of the soil in the fruits of the earth. The working man alone, who has made this garden to 'blossom like the rose, is excluded from its enjoyment. *Hiatus, valde deflendus!* And he is excluded simply because he is not like the horse and the ox, and the sheep, the fish in the pond and the game in the preserves, the property of the owner of the soil. Make him also property, and he would be better fed and cared for than the brutes, for he is more valuable property; and besides, it is more natural for man to love his fellow man, provided that fellow man be his dependant or his master, than it is to love brute creatures. God, when he created the world, established a community of goods, not only between men, but also let in the brute creation to their full share of enjoyment of the fruits of the earth. An attempt has been made in Southern and middle Europe, for the last century or two, to establish a new order of things on the ruins of feudalism, which was a modification of the old order. This attempt has signally failed, as is attested by almost daily revolutions, the starving condition of the working classes, and the general prevalence of socialist doctrines, which doctrines propose the total subversion and re-construction of the social fabric. We entirely agree with the socialists, that free competition is the bane of modern society. We also agree with them, that it is right and necessary to establish in some modified degree, a community of property. We agree with them in the end they propose to attain, and only differ as to the means.

We do not believe that any new discoveries have been made in moral science for the last four thousand years, or that any will hereafter be made. In the remotest antiquity, men had the same lights of experience before them that we have to-day, and they were wiser men and profounder thinkers than we, because their attention was not divided and frittered away, by a thousand objects, wants and pursuits, as ours is, in consequence of the many discoveries in physical science. The ancients led simpler lives, were harrassed by fewer cares, had their minds exercised on fewer subjects, and were therefore wiser men than we. Their works are imperishable, and have a reputation as wide as the world. The fame of the best of ours is ephemeral and local. It is to them we should recur for lessons in government, rather than look to our cotemporaries or indulge in rash experiment. Thousands of years before the days of Moses and Numa, Solon and Lycurgus, the field of experiment had been exhausted, and they no doubt were aware of the results of those experiments, and profited by them.

So little has human nature changed, that we find the men of to-day, with all their virtues and vices, passions and peculiarities, more exactly and faithfully portrayed in the Old Testament, and by the Greek and Latin poets, than by any English or American author of the present day. It is with human nature that government has to deal, and we should look back to thos who understood it best, to learn how to deal with it. The Socialists expect to organise society on entirely new principles. Society every where is much alike and of gradual growth. It is the result of the passions, the motives, the affections, and the selfishness of human nature. These are much the same in all ages and in all countries. What madness and folly, at this late day, to form society for human beings regardless of human nature. Yet the Socialists are guilty of this folly, and gravely propose to change man's nature to fit him for their new institutions. How much more wise, prudent and philosophical it would be to recur to some old tried forms of society, especially as we shall presently show that such forms of society have existed, and do now exist, as will remove all the evils they complain of, and attain all the ends they propose.

A community of property, in some modified degree, existed in all the states of antiquity, whether savage or civilized, and continued to exist under the form of feudalism throughout the dark ages. This community of property existed in two forms. The one form, universal among savages, is where the lands belong to the State and the individuals composing the State have a common right of enjoyment in those lands. Society may get along very happily under this order of things. Nor, indeed, is it wholly inconsistent with the advance of civilization. Every one recollects the example of Sparta, when there was no separate property in lands, and in modern times the Peruvian Indians, the most civilized in America, held their lands in common. The few instances, however, of this kind of community of property among civilized nations, shows that it is adapted only to the savage state. The other kind of community of property, which is at least as old as civilization itself, will require some pains to explain, because we are the first who have treated it in this light. No doubt the same reflections are daily passing through thousands of minds, that now pass through ours, and we but give a new name to an old thought. This latter kind of community of property exists where separate ownership having been acquired in all the soil of a State, those who own that soil own also those individuals who cultivate it. A beautiful example and illustration of this kind of communism, is found in the instance of the Patriarch Abraham. His wives and his children, his men servants and his maid servants, his camels and his cattle, were all equally his property. He could sacrifice Isaac or a ram, just as he pleased. He loved and protected all, and all shared, if not equally, at least fairly, in the products of their light labor. Who would not desire to have been a slave of that old Patriarch, stern and despotic as he was? How quick he would have beheaded a Yankee abolitionist who had abused his open hospitality to entice away his slaves. Poor Hagar! wert thou deluded by some vender of quack medicines and wooden nutmegs? How many Hagars, starving in the wilderness, may now be found at the North? Nay, it is worse than a wilderness to them, for they are surrounded by luxuries which they cannot taste, and by fellow beings whose hideous scowl of hate aggravates their woes. Pride, affection, self-interest, moved Abraham to protect, love and take care of his slaves. The same motives operate on all masters, and secure comfort, competency and protection to the slave. A man's wife and children are his slaves, and do they not enjoy, in common with himself, his property? As he advances in age and his wants become fewer, his chil-

dren most always get the lion's share. Look to a well
ordered farm and see whether the cattle, the horses, the
sheep, and the hogs, do not enjoy their full proportion
of the proceeds of the farm. Would you emancipate
them too? Why not? Liberty and idleness are as
natural and agreeable to them as to slaves.

Men love the brute creatures that belong to them.
It is the law of God impressed on the heart of man
that secures good and kind treatment to the brutes, far
more effectually than all human law can do. The same
law of God makes man love his slaves far more than
he does his horse. The affection which all men feel
for what belongs to them, and for what is dependent
on them, is Nature's magna charta, which shields, protects and provides for wives, children and slaves. The
selfishness of man's nature, which occasions all the
oppression of the weak by the powerful, the poor by
the rich, in free society, is the very instrument which
Providence in his wisdom has chosen to protect the
weak and the poor in a natural and healthy state of
society—that is in a society where domestic slavery exists. Ye meddlesome, profane, presumptuous abolition-
its! think ye that God has done his work imperfectly
and needs your aid? He that takes account of the
sparrow, has he no care for the slave? Is he waiting,
and has he waited for four thousand years, for you to
do his work? Must you steal the negro before he
can save his soul? Are not the negroes whom you
have stolen and freed, ten times more vicious than our
slaves? Has God permitted slavery to exist so long
and so generally, because he knew no better, or be-

cause he was afraid to denounce it, or was he waiting for you to help him?

In the February No. of the North British Review, in a critique on Sir Charles Lyell's Travels in North America, we find the following singular and contradictory language. We say contradictory, for if "self-interest and domestic feeling combine to surround the slave with every blessing," what becomes of the "cruelty and injustice," the "sound of the whip and the clank of the chain?" Does domestic feeling exhibit itself in this way?

"Could we look at the slave in his simple humanity, without regarding him as a being of the future, we should view him as the inmate of a luxurious house, with all the blessings with which self-interest and domestic feeling combine to surround him. Under this bright phase, and in striking contrast with the in-dweller of the work-house, or the laborer in the factory, we are disposed to forget the horrors of the middle passage, and shut our ears to the sound of the whip and the clank of the chain. But when the mind's eye rests upon the precious jewel—the white soul which the clay cask encloses—eternal truth recoils from the sight of a spirit in shackles, and immortal affection clasps in her warmest embrace the victims of cruelty and injustice."

We suppose the writer thinks there are no slaves in heaven, but plenty of savages, cannibals and free negroes. "The Devil can quote scripture for his purpose," but we think this would puzzle him.

If any doubt our theory, that domestic slavery does establish a fair community of goods, we cite them to the facts. Look to the old Patriarchs and their slaves, to the feudal lords and their vassals, or come to the South and see our farms. See the aged and infirm, the women and children, on every farm, more tenderly watched over and better provided for, than the sturdy and laborious. God intended, no doubt, that those who most needed sympathy, assistance and attention, should have most of it. Put your own house in order, ye abolitionists? When the women and children, the sick and the aged, in your laboring class, are secure of the same ample provision, sympathy and attention as our slaves, then, and not till then, offer your advice to us.

But we have said the slave is secure of a *fair* proportion of the profits in the community of property which grows out of the institution of domestic slavery. We will explain how this happens, and cite facts to prove that it is so. As man rises in the scale of civilization his wants increase, his skill and capacity for production increase pari passu. As a slave, he needs more and is entitled to more, of the products of the joint concern, than the mere newly imported savage. As he assimilates himself to his master, his master's attachment to him increases; he is made a mechanic, a dining-room or body servant, and is treated very differently from what we call "out hands." Each, however, has his wants supplied. The negroes first imported to this country were badly clad; clothes to them were an irksome incumbrance. Our male field hands even now generally prefer a bench by the fire and a blanket, to the finest feather bed in the world. They are but gradually learning to like plank floors to their houses. The masters are more ready to supply their wants than they are to acquire them.

There is another law of our nature that secures to the slave his right. Place men in the relation of master and slave, and the wiser and more strong willed invariably rules. It is so in the case of man and wife, father and child, and slaves have often been "a power behind the throne greater than the throne itself," and thus ruled empires. Negroes do not rule their masters, because of the inferiority of race, but they are better treated as they advance in morality and intelligence.

Besides that domestic slavery does away with competition, so ruinous to the working classes in free countries, and occasions a community of profits if not of property—it supplies another great desideratum of the socialists, and, indeed, of the political economists too: it brings about the ASSOCIATION OF LABOR. This result, too, is obtained in a better form than any we have seen suggested by the Socialists. They propose only to associate men of the same trade. Domestic slavery profitably associates men, women and children, mechanics and common laborers. On a farm, under the supervision of one master, who supplies the skill and capital, all ages and sexes can find appropriate and profitable employment. Set the slaves on a farm free, and leave each to get employment, and however disposed to work, the products of their labor would not sit half what they were before. Much time must be lost in looking for work, and they would rarely find beuations where all the members of a large family could get employment. Much loss would ensue from the want of one common head to find them work and give skillful direction to their labor, and still more from the fact that each one buying for himself, their wants would be supplied at retail instead of wholesale prices.

This association of labor and capital, by means of domestic slavery, would remove another evil that bewilders, staggers and confounds Malthusians, Economists and Socialists alike. This is the evil of excessive population, an evil sorely felt through half of Europe, and irremediable because confined to the most indigent who have no means of emigrating. If they were slaves, their masters would send them at once to countries where population was sparse and labor dear; and they would be sent off in families, not separated as free people generally are when they remove. Thus is slavery the simple and adequate remedy for the greatest evil with which mankind is afflicted at present or threatened for the future.

We cannot believe that the Socialists do not see that domestic slavery is the only practicable form of socialism—they are afraid yet to pronounce the word.

An admirable proof and illustration of our doctrine, that slavery is communism, might be had by making all the working-men in England slaves to the land-holders, and requiring by law the land-holders to support them as we do our slaves. Would not, in such case, the working-men be joint owners of the farm? If the land-holders were also permitted to sell them, or remove them to the colonies where labor is scarce and dear, it would be an excellent bargain on both sides. Labor and capital would thus be beneficially associated. They do sell white men now in England, and remove them to distant colonies, but require as a perquisite to the boon, that a man should first steal a turnip or shoot a hare· Many take the boon even on these harsh terms, rather than starve; they steal in order to be shipped to New Holland and sold as slaves. They are willing to encounter the disgrace of crime, and be torn from every tie of friendship and affection, rather than remain in England and starve. Could the poor of England sell themselves and families for terms of years, or for life, or in perpetuity, they would at once have the means of certain and comfortable support. Removed to new colonies, they might by extra work and frugality, soon purchase their liberty again. The situation of the slave is a good one to amass money, because he may save all he makes, the master supplying all his wants.

We have often been reminded of the absurdity of the law which prevents a man's selling himself, or to speak more accurately, which refuses to enforce performance of the contract, whilst observing the character of the emigration to California. No poor man could get to the mines, except by deserting the army, the navy, or the merchant service. The law permitted him to sell his liberty for five years, and subject himself to hard fare and harsh treatment, and low wages, provided he would enter either of those services. He might sell himself for eight dollars a month, and have the cat applied to his back gratis once a quarter, but he might not sell himself for fifty dollars per month to work in the mines and be well treated. The law, we know, is the perfection of reason, and liberty the greatest good, yet we can't help thinking, when a strong young fellow finds his whole capital reduced to his own person, it would be as well to let him pawn that or sell it, "to make a raise." It is the only way a poor fellow can get a start in life sometimes, and it seems hard to prohibit his using, in the way of trade, the only capital he has left. We wonder it never occurred to the economists, who so much admire free trade and free competition, that the denial of this right was part of the restrictive and protective system. Laissez nous faire! Let us sell ourselves if we please!

That the condition of working men, in all old countries where population is dense, is a thousand times worse than that of our slaves, is a FACT that no one will dispute. This *fact* is worth all the theories in the world, and shows conclusively that the common laborers should be slaves, in old countries. It is hard for us Americans to understand why this must ever be so, for here population is generally sparse, and working men scarce; so that working men are in demand and can get just such wages as they choose to demand. Mrs. Trollope, by far the most philosophical traveller who has visited America, very justly remarked, that the difficulty of retaining a servant in Cincinnati, showed that there the master or employer was under obligations to the servant. The servant might work one day in the week and get enough wages to live on all the week; the master needed a servant every day and could with difficulty get one, because masters were more numerous than servants. The COMPETITION was among masters to get servants, not among servants to get places. This competition of course continually increased the wages of servants. We will venture the assertion, based upon mere theory, that this state of things is already changed in Ohio—servants have become more numerous than employers. There is already competition and under-bidding to get places, because population is dense; and we will stake our reputation, that the white servants in Cincinnati are not as well paid as our negro slaves. We mean that their wages are not sufficient to secure to them and their families the same comforts in all seasons of the year, in health, and in sickness, as we allow our slaves. In a newly and partially settled country like California, working men have greatly the advantage over mere moneyed men, and slavery is not necessary for their protection. Competition in such countries is attended with no evils, and greatly promotes the rapid development of its resources. In settling a new country, free labor is better than slave labor, because competition stimulates industry, without impairing the condition of the laborer. In old countries, every stimulant to increased industry is an injury to the laboring class, for thereby a few do the work that should employ many, and thus leave the many to starve. In old countries, human wisdom can devise no effectual means to provide for the poor, where lands have become separate property, except by making slaves of those who hold no property to those who have property, and thus in fact, if not in form, establishing a community of property. The history of the free States of Europe, for the last sixty years, and the present condition of the poor in those States, we think conclusively proves this. All parties admit that society there requires radical change. They must go back to domestic slavery. Civilized society cannot long exist without it. In conclusion, we will sum up the evidence that establishes this truth beyond doubt, independent of all theory. In the slave States of this Union all classes of society are satisfied with government as it is; famine is neither known nor apprehended, and there is no complaint that the wages of the working class are inadequate to their comfortable support. In the whole South there is not one Socialist, not one man, rich or poor, proposing to subvert and re-construct society. Society is in a natural, healthy and contented state. Such was very much the condition of society in middle and southern Europe two centuries ago, before feudalism disappeared and liberty and equality were established. Now, in these latter countries, famine and revolutions. are daily occurrences; the poor are discontented, riotous and insurrectionary, and the rich, from mere sympathy with the sufferings of the poor, have become young English men, Chartists and Socialists, and admit that the organization of society is wholly wrong, and the sufferings of the poor intolerable. What more proof is needed, that the diseases that afflict society with them are occasioned by the absence of domestic slavery, and what remedy so obvious as to remove the cause of those diseases by restoring that institution?

CONTENTS.

589643

Life
Bc. 729
14 -70

APPENDIX.

Made in the USA
Middletown, DE
06 November 2024

63996743R00175